CONTENTS

PREFACE

Many of the managers and executives who attend short management accounting courses, and students involved with non-professional accountancy courses, frequently comment that:

☐ They don't want to become accountants.
☐ They have no desire to become expert in the number-crunching side of accountancy.

However, they do all appear to have a good idea about what they are really looking for. I have been told on numerous occasions by managers, executives and non-professional accountancy students that what they need to be able to do is the following:

☐ Acquire a good grasp of the terminology used.
☐ Acquire a working knowledge of the important principles and techniques.
☐ Understand how the figures that are produced have been arrived at, e.g. how the overhead cost of a product may be calculated.
☐ Know what information could be available to assist with decision making.
☐ Use the information that is generated.
☐ Know about the limitations of the information produced.
☐ Appreciate the way in which the information, systems and techniques may affect people, i.e. the behavioural aspects.

Readership

This book has been especially written for managers and executives attending short courses, for reading either before or during the course. However, students undertaking business and management courses of a longer duration should also find the book helpful as pre-course reading or revision or for reading during their course; e.g. it should be particularly useful for one-semester introductory-level undergraduate degree courses and postgraduate courses such as the MA and MBA.

Teaching and learning features

☐ Each chapter sets out the objectives which it is intended will have been achieved by the time the study of the chapter has been completed.
☐ It is written in a clear and concise user-friendly style.

☐ The worked examples in the text, which illustrate management accounting techniques, take the reader through the process, step by step.

☐ Integrated throughout the text are several self-assessment questions, with suggested answers given at the end of the text.

☐ A summary of key points is provided at the end of each chapter.

☐ Each chapter ends with some suggested further reading.

The author welcomes comments from users of this book which will be taken into account when a new edition is prepared, and would like to thank all those users who commented on the earlier editions.

1

Introduction to management accounting

The principal aim of this chapter is to introduce you to the purpose and scope of management accounting. When you have completed this chapter you should be able to do the following:

☐ Appreciate why predetermined cost and management accounting systems are needed.
☐ Understand what is meant by elements of cost.
☐ Distinguish between direct and indirect costs, and fixed and variable costs.
☐ Appreciate the way in which management accounting can meet the needs of management.

Cost and management accounting systems

Cost and management accounting systems can be divided into two, as shown in Figure 1.1. Historic costing looks back at past performance. However, it must be remembered that simply comparing current performance with past performance is not such a satisfactory way of controlling business activities.

Why not? Because it is hard to say whether or not past performance has been good, bad or indifferent.

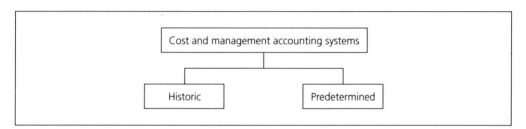

Figure 1.1 Cost and management accounting

However, management accounting tends to make extensive use of predetermined systems such as budgetary control and standard costing.

Why? The principal reasons are as follows:

☐ A lot of the management accounting information produced is about the future. Management needs to be able to assess what its decisions/proposed decisions will mean in terms of future costs and revenues, etc.

☐ The quest for a 'yardstick', i.e. a way of assessing and measuring performance, e.g. a sales target, budgeted expenditure on advertising, etc.

The budgets and standards used should provide targets at which to aim; they should *not* merely reflect what is expected to happen. Thus, control can be exercised by comparing the planned (budgets or standards) figures with the actual results at regular intervals.

The elements of cost

The cost of a product, job or service is made up of the elements of cost, i.e. materials, labour and overheads (see Figure 1.2). The last of the three (overheads) is the most difficult to deal with. In later chapters we will look at how overheads are dealt with in total absorption costing, activity based costing and marginal costing.

Figure 1.2 The elements of cost

The classification of costs

Costs can be classified in a number of ways (see Figure 1.3):

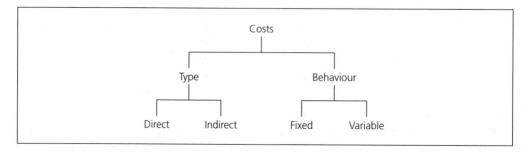

Figure 1.3 The classification of costs

☐ **Direct costs** can be identified as forming part of the product or service, e.g. manufacturing wages and raw materials which are used in the production process.

☐ **Indirect costs** are usually referred to as **overheads**; they are expenses which do not form part of the product or service, e.g. the wages of cleaners and canteen staff, materials used for cleaning, and maintenance.

☐ **Fixed costs** have to be paid out irrespective of the level of activity, but within a relevant range. Examples are insurance of buildings, rent of premises and maintenance contracts.

☐ **Variable (marginal) costs** comprise the direct costs referred to above plus variable overheads. They may be described as those costs which vary with the level of activity within a relevant range. Examples of variable costs are direct materials plus those expenses which vary with the level of output, e.g. power for machines.

A combination of fixed and variable costs may be referred to as a **semi-variable** cost, e.g. a fixed rental for some equipment plus a variable element charged according to usage.

Costs may be further divided up between products, services, departments, sections and functions. These may be referred to as **cost centres**. A cost centre is simply a location, person or function, etc., to which costs are allocated and apportioned. The aim is to collect and accumulate the costs applicable to each specific cost centre.

What is management accounting?

Management accounting is very closely linked to cost accounting; so closely, in fact, that it is difficult to say where cost accounting ends and where management accounting begins. **Cost accounting** simply aims to measure the performance of departments, goods and services. However, **management accounting** is much, much more, and involves the following.

☐ *The provision of information for management*
Indeed, the role of the management accountant could well be described as that of an 'information manager'. The information generated should be designed to assist management, to control business operations, and to help management with decision making. In fulfilling this role the management accounting department/section must consult with the users of the information, i.e. management, to assess their needs in terms of precisely what information is required and when, etc. The aim is to provide management with a flow of relevant information, e.g. reports, statements, spreadsheets, etc., as and when required. A frequent flow of information (weekly or monthly) should enable management to respond to emerging problems/situations as soon as possible. The early detection of problems means earlier solutions and early action.

☐ *Advising management*
A key part of management accounting is to advise management about the economic consequences and implications of its (proposed) decisions and alternative courses of action. In particular, this advice should answer a frequently overlooked question: **what**

happens if things go wrong, or if interest rates go up, or if the sales target is not achieved?

☐ *Forecasting, planning and control*
A lot of management accounting is concerned with the future and with predetermined systems such as budgetary control and standard costing. Such systems investigate the differences (i.e. variances) which arise as a result of actual performance being different from planned performance. In addition, the management accountant should also be involved in strategic planning, e.g. the setting of objectives and the formulation of policy. The forecasting process will involve accounting for uncertainty (risk) via statistical techniques, such as probability, etc.

☐ *Communications*
If the management accounting system is to be really effective it is essential that it goes hand in hand with a good, sound, reliable and efficient communication system. Such a system should communicate clearly by providing information in a form which the user, e.g. managers and their subordinates, can easily understand (reports, statements, tabulations, graphs and charts). However, great care should be taken to ensure that managers do not suffer from 'information overload', i.e. having too much information, much of which they could well do without!

☐ *Systems*
The management accounting department/section will also be actively involved with the design of cost control systems and financial reporting systems.

☐ *Flexibility*
Management accounting should be flexible enough to respond quickly to changes in the environment in which the company/organization operates. Where necessary the information/systems and budgets etc. should be amended/modified. Thus, there is a need for the management accounting section/department to be involved with the monitoring of the environment on a continuing basis.

☐ *An appreciation of other business functions*
Those who provide management accounting information need to understand the role played by the other business functions. In addition to communicating effectively with other business functions, they may also need to secure their cooperation and coordination, e.g. the budget preparation process relies on the existence of good communications, cooperation and coordination.

☐ *Staff education*
The management accounting department/section needs to ensure that all the users of the information it provides, e.g. managers and their subordinates, are educated about the techniques used, their purpose and their benefits, etc.

☐ *'Gate-keeping'*
The management accounting department/section sits at a very important information junction (see Figure 1.4). This gate-keeping position places the management accounting section in a position of power; it has access to (can send information to and from)

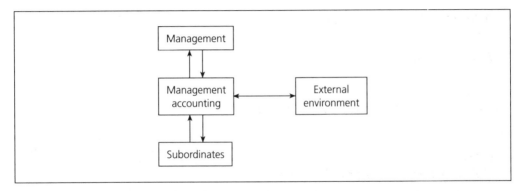

Figure 1.4 Management accounting: the gate-keeper

management and subordinates, and communicates with and receives a certain amount of information from the external environment. Its power arises because it can control the flow of information upwards to management or downwards to subordinates.

☐ *Limitations*
Although management accounting can, and does, provide a lot of useful information, it must be stressed that this is *not* an exact science. A vast amount of the information generated depends upon subjective judgement, e.g. the assessment of qualitative factors or assumptions about the business environment. Management accounting is not the be-all-and-end-all of decision making – it is just one of the tools which can help management to make more informed decisions.

☐ *Being the servant*
Finally, having established that management accounting is a tool, it must be emphasized that it is there to serve the needs of management.

Summary: an introduction to management accounting

Cost and management accounting systems
☐ **Historic** looks backwards at past events.
☐ **Predetermined** looks forward to the future.

Management accounting makes extensive use of predetermined systems such as budgetary control and standard costing.

The elements of cost
☐ Materials.
☐ Labour.
☐ Overheads.

The classification of costs

☐ Direct or indirect.
☐ Fixed or variable.

The role of management accounting

Management accounting attempts to provide managers and executives with a regular supply of relevant information which will enable them to manage more effectively, efficiently and economically. It also involves:

☐ Advising management about the possible consequences of its actions.
☐ Forecasting, planning and control.
☐ Communications.
☐ Systems.
☐ Flexibility.
☐ An appreciation of other business functions.
☐ Staff education.
☐ 'Gate keeping'.
☐ Limitations.
☐ Being the servant and 'information manager' of the management.

Management accounting should thus assist management with decision making and problem solving. It should help managers and executives to make the best use of their valuable time and talents in fulfilling their responsibilities and enable them to take advantage of emerging opportunities.

Further reading

Drury, C., *Costing: An Introduction*, International Thomson Business Press, 1998.
Dyson, J., *Accounting for Non-accounting Students*, Financial Times Pitman, 2000.
Weetman, P., *Management Accounting*, Financial Times Prentice Hall, 1999.

2

Materials

Objectives

When you have worked through this chapter you should be able to do the following:

☐ Appreciate how the FIFO (first in, first out), LIFO (last in, first out) and AVECO (average cost) methods of pricing materials issued to production actually work.
☐ Also understand how they can affect product costs and stock valuations.
☐ Remember the kind of information which the management accounting section can produce to assist with the effective management and control of materials.

Note that it is not the objective of this chapter that you become an expert in the computational side of stock valuations. However, further reading is recommended at the end of the chapter for those who wish to delve deeper into the subject.

The valuation of materials

Materials need to be valued for the following two purposes:

☐ Product costs.
☐ Stock valuations.

There are numerous methods which may be applied for cost and management accounting purposes. We will look at three of them, which are as follows:

☐ FIFO: first in, first out.
☐ LIFO: last in, first out.
☐ AVECO: average cost.

We shall now use Example 2.1 to illustrate how they work. For each of the three methods, we can look at the calculations involved and the effect on both product costs and stock valuations.

Example 2.1 The valuation of materials

We have been provided with the following information relating to the stock of component ZYX 3964 in 20X2:

> 1 April: opening stock b/f (brought forward) 500 units at £10 each.
> 7 April: received from suppliers 1,000 units at £12 each.
> 9 April: issued to production 200 units.
> 23 April: issued to production 400 units.

FIFO (first in, first out)

This method values the material issued to production according to the order in which it arrived, as shown in Table 2.1. It can be observed that all issues are priced at the first price of £10 until all of the 500 units opening stock, which had come in at that price, had been covered. Having dealt with the 500 opening stock units, all other issues up to the 1,000 which came in next will be priced at £12 per unit.

Table 2.1 Example of FIFO method of valuing material

20X2		Units			Value £
1 April		500	Opening stock b/f @ £10		5,000
7 April	*plus*	1,000	Received @ £12		12,000
		1,500	Stock in hand		17,000
9 April	*less*	200	Issued @ £10		2,000
		1,300	Stock in hand		15,000
				£	
			Issued 300 @ £10	3,000	
23 April	*less*	400	100 @ £12	1,200	4,200
		900	**Closing stock**		**10,800**
			Summary	Units	£
			Value of stock b/f and received	1,500	17,000
	less		Value of stock issued to		
			production (£2,000 + £4,200)	600	6,200
			Value of closing stock		
			(900 @ £12)	900	10,800

In times of rising prices this method has the effect of including the older, lower prices in the product costs and the higher, more recent prices in the stock-in-hand valuations. However, it does follow the order in which the stock should be physically issued, i.e. the stock should be issued in the order in which it arrived so as to avoid losses caused by ageing/deterioration.

Table 2.2 Example of LIFO method of valuing material

20X2		Units			Value £
1 April		500	Opening stock b/f @ £10		5,000
7 April	*plus*	1,000	Received @ £12		12,000
		1,500	Stock in hand		17,000
9 April	*less*	200	Issued @ £12		2,400
		1,300	Stock in hand		14,600
23 April	*less*	400	Issued @ £12		4,800
		900	**Closing stock**		**9,800**

		Summary	Units	£
		Value of stock b/f and received	1,500	17,000
	less	Value of stock issued to		
		production (£2,400 + £4,800)	600	7,200
		Value of closing stock	900	9,800

Table 2.3 Closing stock valuation using LIFO

	£
Closing stock = 400 units at £12	4,800
500 units @ £10	5,000
	9,800

LIFO (last in, first out)

The LIFO method values material issued to production at the most recent price as shown in Table 2.2.

The closing stock represents the 400 units which remain of the units which were purchased on 7 April at £12 per unit and the 500 opening stock units at £10 per unit, as shown in Table 2.3.

Any further issues, provided that no new stock is received, will be valued at £12 per unit up to the 400 units remaining and then at £10 per unit.

The LIFO method is not in line with the method by which the stock should be physically issued (i.e. FIFO). However, in times of rising prices, it does charge the higher, more recent prices to product costs, leaving the older, lower prices in the closing stock valuation. Thus, the product costs are more realistic and reflect current prices; however, the closing stock valuation will be understated, not being at current prices.

AVECO (average cost)

With the AVECO method (see Table 2.4), all the issues and stock are valued at the average price. The average price will be recomputed every time a new batch of materials is received from suppliers.

Thus, all issues are priced at £11.33p and the closing stock is valued at £11.33p per unit. However, note that 900 units at £11.33 = £10,197, *not* £10,202. This is caused by **rounding** the average cost per unit to the nearest penny.

Table 2.4 Example of AVECO method of valuing material

20X2		Units		Value £
1 April		500	Opening stock b/f @ £10	5,000.00
7 April	plus	1,000	Received @ £12	12,000.00
		1,500	Stock in hand	17,000.00
9 April	less	200	Issued @ £11.33*	2,266.00
		1,300	Stock in hand	14,734.00
23 April	less	400	Issued @ £11.33	4,532.00
		900	**Closing stock @ £11.33**	**10,202.00**

$$* \text{ Note: The average cost} = \frac{£17,000}{1,500 \text{ units}} = £11.33 \text{ (to the nearest penny)}.$$

The advantage claimed for this method is that all products, are for a time, charged for the same material at a uniform rate.

Managerial considerations

From a management point of view, you must appreciate that:

☐ With the exception of FIFO these are not methods by which materials are to be physically issued, but merely methods for the pricing of materials issued to production and for ascertaining the valuation of stocks on hand. For example, although we may use LIFO or AVECO for pricing purposes, the materials involved should still be physically issued on a FIFO basis to avoid losses caused by the ageing process, etc.

☐ They will produce different results in terms of product costs and stock valuations, e.g. see the figures illustrated in Table 2.5.

☐ The figures will be affected by price fluctuations, the quantities received and issued and the frequency of those receipts and issues.

☐ There are other methods which can be used, e.g. standard cost or replacement cost, highest in first out (HIFO), next in first out (NIFO).

Table 2.5 Stock valuation: comparison of product costs and closing stock valuations

	Product costs £	Closing stock £
FIFO (£2,000 + £4,200)	6,200	10,800
LIFO (£2,400 + £4,800)	7,200	9,800
AVECO (£2,266 + £4,532)	6,798	10,202

Summary: materials

The valuation of materials

There are a number of valuation methods which can be used for the pricing of materials issued to production and for stock valuation purposes.

FIFO (first in, first out)

This method prices issues to products by following the sequence in which the stock arrived. This means that the material element of the product cost is at an earlier price, whether it be lower or higher than the price at which the material concerned has subsequently been bought. The stock valuation reflects the more recent price.

LIFO (last in, first out)

The effect on product costs and stock valuations is opposite from that produced by the FIFO (first in, first out) method.

AVECO (average cost)

There are a number of variations of this method which can be used. The method which we have looked at recomputes the average cost every time a new delivery of stock is received, as follows:

$$\text{average cost} = \frac{\text{balance of stock b/f} + \text{value of new stock received}}{\text{total number of units}}$$

$$\text{e.g.} \quad \frac{£5,000 + £12,000}{500 \text{ units} + 1,000 \text{ units}} = \frac{£17,000}{1,500 \text{ units}} = £11.33\text{p per unit}$$

Only the FIFO (first in, first out) method is in line with the recommended way in which the materials should be physically used. All other methods are, therefore, purely methods of pricing. Remember that different methods of pricing are quite likely to produce significantly varying results.

Further reading

Hussey, J. and Hussey, R., *Cost and Management Accounting*, Macmillan, 1998.
Storey, R., *Introduction to Cost and Management Accounting*, Macmillan, 1995.

3

Labour

Objectives

When you have read carefully through this chapter, you should be able to appreciate the following:

☐ The importance of the payroll analysis and the idle time analysis in the provision of management accounting information.
☐ Some of the causes of idle (or non-productive) time.
☐ How attendance time can be reconciled.
☐ The kind of management accounting data which can be produced via incentive schemes.
☐ What is meant by 'labour turnover'.
☐ Which costs should be included in the cost of labour turnover.
☐ What management can do to reduce the cost of labour turnover.
☐ The need for information about recent and future developments in the labour market.

Payroll analysis

One of the principal means of providing cost and management accounting information is the payroll analysis. Both direct and indirect workers can record how they spend their time via time sheets, clock cards and computer keyboards, etc.

Direct workers will record how much time they spend producing products or working on jobs or the provision of a service, and how much of their time is non-productive (i.e. idle). Thus, the payroll analysis will be able to provide labour costs per product, job, department or section. This will enable comparisons to be made with budgets and/or standards and the reporting of variances. It will also provide valuable information which should assist with the task of producing budgets for future accounting periods.

Another aspect of payroll analysis is **idle (non-productive) time analysis**. This analysis will show how many hours are lost for each specific reason. Some of the causes of idle time are as follows:

☐ Waiting for materials.
☐ Waiting for work.
☐ Waiting for the setter.

☐ Machine breakdown.
☐ Training a new operative.
☐ Committee meetings, etc.

To become more efficient management must strive to reduce idle (non-productive, lost) time.

The attendance time of direct workers can be reconciled thus:

attendance time recorded = productive time recorded + idle time recorded

As mentioned earlier, indirect workers, e.g. cleaners, welfare and maintenance staff, can keep a record of how and where they spend their time. The payroll analysis will therefore include an analysis of indirect labour per department or section. This analysis should prove useful in the estimation of the predetermined indirect labour budget figure which is needed for computing departmental overhead absorption rates (see Chapter 4). The analysis of indirect labour can also be used to compare with budgeted figures for control purposes, e.g. to see if any overspending has occurred.

Incentive schemes

The management accounting section can provide useful information relating to incentive schemes:

☐ A comparison between proposed schemes.
☐ The effects of amendments to existing schemes.
☐ Productivity records.

Management accounting is also concerned with the monitoring of existing incentive schemes.

The cost of labour turnover

Management needs to be more aware of the real cost of employing people, i.e. the cost of labour turnover.

What is labour turnover? It is the rate at which people leave an employer, and may be calculated as follows:

$$\frac{\text{number of persons leaving}}{\text{average number of persons on the payroll}} \times 100 \quad \text{(for, say, per month, quarter or half year)}$$

See for example, Table 3.1.

Table 3.1 The rate of labour turnover

Quarter	No. of persons who left	Average no. on payroll	Rate of labour turnover %
1	17	85	20.00
2	19	114	16.67

Which costs should be included? The short answer to this question is 'a lot more than you would expect to see'. Labour turnover could include the following costs:

☐ Advertising vacancies.

☐ Recruitment – including the cost of drawing up job specifications and the employment of specialist recruitment agencies.

☐ Selection – interviews in terms of the personnel involved and the facilities provided, the hire of accommodation, meals, refreshments, travelling expenses, etc. Where special selection tests are used there are costs associated with their design, development, testing, monitoring, marking, administration and review.

☐ Engagement – records, medicals, special clothing and equipment needs.

☐ The personnel function – in terms of salaries, offices, fixtures, fittings and equipment and associated overheads such as light and heat, printing, stationery, telephone costs, etc.

☐ Training costs, e.g. induction training (courses for new employees to inform them about the company/organization and its products/services), pre-job training in the company's/organization's own training school, courses, text books, travelling expenses, etc.

☐ Production costs, such as lost production of those who are supervising the work of new operatives. There is also the likelihood of a reduced level of output and a higher level of defective output from new operatives.

☐ Morale and motivation – these are both difficult to quantify but can have a dramatic impact upon the company/organization and its products/services.

What can be done to reduce the cost of labour turnover? Management needs to know the rate of labour turnover and the reasons why people leave. Managers should, therefore, obtain the rate of labour turnover:

☐ Per department or section.

☐ For males and females in age groups.

They need to find out why people are leaving and analyse whether the reasons are controllable or uncontrollable. This kind of information can be collected via interviews or questionnaires by the personnel department. Employees could leave for any of the following reasons:

☐ Pay.

☐ The nature of the work.

☐ Promotion.

☐ The hours.

☐ Working conditions.

☐ Relationships with superiors and/or subordinates.

☐ Housing and/or transport problems.

☐ Welfare and social considerations.

☐ Health.

☐ Moving away from the area.

It can be seen that the process of employing people entails a great deal more than simply engaging them and paying them a wage or salary. There are many, many costs involved in the employment of labour. In fact, it can be said in conclusion that the cost of employing people represents a significant investment and that the cost of labour turnover is far greater than a lot of people would imagine.

Other matters

Quite recent and future developments in the labour area will continue to make demands upon the management accounting section. The implications of the following will all need to be costed, analysed, compared with appropriate data and monitored:

☐ Productivity deals.

☐ The introduction of flexitime.

☐ The provision of a nursery for employees' children.

☐ Profit-sharing schemes.

☐ Employees' share schemes.

☐ Executives/designers, etc., working from home via computer links.

☐ Corporate incentives, e.g. holidays for sales staff, etc.

You should now appreciate why we described the management accounting function in our opening chapter as that of an information provider/manager.

Summary: labour

Payroll analysis

The payroll can be divided into two categories.

Direct labour
Labour used to transform the raw material into finished goods or for the provision of a service. The direct labour content of a product/service can be ascertained via the time recording system, by e.g. time sheets, time cards and computer systems as a by-product of the payroll analysis.

Indirect labour
Non-manufacturing workers and those not directly involved in providing a service, such as cleaners, welfare workers, canteen staff and maintenance personnel, can also record how they spend their time via time sheets or time cards, etc. It should therefore be possible to produce a payroll analysis for the indirect workers, per department or section, etc.

Another important part of payroll analysis is the idle (non-productive) time analysis. This should direct the attention of management to the areas in which hours are being lost so that, where possible, corrective action can be taken which should help to remedy the situation.

The payroll analysis can be a considerable help during the budget preparation period and with the setting of standards.

Incentive schemes

Management needs to be provided with information such as updates of existing schemes, comparative figures for new schemes and productivity records.

The cost of labour turnover

This is a cost which tends to be overlooked/ignored by management; but it is a cost which does/can involve huge sums of money:

$$\text{the rate of labour turnover} = \frac{\text{number of persons leaving}}{\text{average number of persons on the payroll}} \times 100$$

This is calculated on, say, a monthly, quarterly or half-yearly basis. It represents the rate at which employees leave a particular employer.

The costs associated with the employment of the labour force are:

☐ Administrative, e.g. advertising, recruitment, selection, engagement and the personnel function.
☐ Training, e.g. induction training, training courses, own training schools.
☐ Production, e.g. losses caused by new employees and defective production.
☐ Damage to morale and motivation.

Management needs to ensure that records are kept of why employees leave and that controllable causes are investigated so that appropriate corrective action may be taken.

Further thoughts

Management accounting information will be needed for both current and future developments in the labour area, e.g. to assess the impact on costs of providing nursery places for employees' children or allowing certain executives/designers, etc., to work at home via computer links.

Further reading

Drury, C., *Costing: An Introduction*, International Thomson Business Press, 1998.
Weetman, P., *Management Accounting*, Financial Times Prentice Hall, 1999.

4

Total absorption costing

Objectives

By the time you have finished studying this chapter, you should be able to do the following:

☐ Understand how overheads are incorporated into the cost of a job, product or service.
☐ Prepare an overhead distribution summary and calculate:
  ● a machine hour rate;
  ● a direct labour hour rate;
  ● the cost of a job, product or service.
☐ Appreciate the limitations of total absorption costing.

The aim of total absorption costing

The principal aim of total absorption costing (also called **absorption costing** or **total costing** or the **full cost method**) is to attempt to ensure that all overhead costs are covered by the revenues received. It should be mentioned here that this is *not an attempt to produce accurate costs*. It is, however, an attempt to answer the question of how much should be included for overheads in costing jobs, products or services.

Overheads

Overheads comprise the indirect expenditure of a business, i.e. that expenditure which does not form part of the product, job or service and includes such costs as:

☐ **Indirect labour**: cleaners, canteen staff, security staff, supervisory staff, etc.
☐ **Indirect materials**: e.g. cleaning materials, maintenance materials, etc.
☐ **Indirect expenses**: rent, insurance of buildings, heating, lighting, etc.

The overheads can also be subdivided into fixed overheads and variable overheads.

Cost centres

Cost centre is the name given to a unit/section to which costs are allocated and apportioned. It could be a department, a process, a function, a service, a group of machines or a person. The aim is to arrive at a total overhead cost for each cost centre. All organizations/companies, including those which provide a service, e.g. the BBC, banking, insurance, education, may have numerous cost centres.

You may also come across the term **profit centre**. This is much the same as a cost centre, but is also revenue-earning. Thus, a profit or loss for the centre can be computed.

Overhead absorption

Overhead absorption (also called **overhead recovery**) is the process of sharing out the overheads between jobs, products or services by means of **absorption rates/recovery rates**, e.g. a rate per direct labour hour or a rate per machine hour.

Absorption costing differs from marginal costing (which we will look at in Chapter 6) in that it attempts to include most of the overheads in product, job or service costs. Marginal costing, on the other hand, includes only the variable overheads in product costs.

We will now describe how a typical absorption costing system in a manufacturing environment works by reference to the absorption of overheads diagram (see Figure 4.1). Because the overheads have to be charged to jobs/products/services throughout the period/year, the recovery rates must be calculated before the period/year begins, i.e. they have to be predetermined.

Stage 1
The production overheads, i.e. the indirect materials, labour and expenses have to be estimated for the forthcoming period/year.

Stage 2
Those overheads which can be identified with and traced to a department/cost centre are charged to the department/cost centre concerned, i.e. they are *allocated* to the cost centre.

Stage 3
Overheads which cannot be allocated to cost centres, i.e. those which cannot be identified and traced to departments/cost centres will have to be *apportioned* to departments/cost centres using some arbitrary basis. A number of overheads tend to *vary more with time than output* and will have to be shared out between the cost centres using some method of apportionment (see Table 4.1).

Stage 4
Having collected all the overheads applicable to the service departments, the total overhead cost of each service department can be shared out between the user departments/

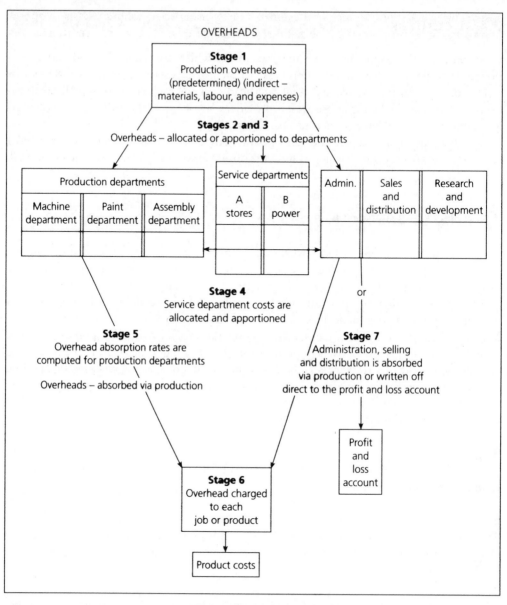

Figure 4.1 Absorption costing in a manufacturing environment

Table 4.1 The apportionment of overheads

Item of overhead expenditure	Basis of apportionment
Rent/heating	Floor area or cubic capacity
Supervision/canteen	Number of employees

costs centres according to technical estimates or by using some arbitrary basis of apportionment, e.g. in proportion to the number of issue notes for the stores department.

Stage 5
The overhead absorption (overhead recovery) rates are calculated. The total overhead for each production department, inclusive of its share of service department costs, is divided by the estimated machine hours or direct labour hours, as appropriate:

$$\frac{\text{machine department overheads}}{\text{estimated no. of machine hours}} = \text{the rate per machine hour}$$

$$\frac{\text{paint department overheads}}{\text{estimated no. of direct labour hours}} = \text{the rate per direct labour hour}$$

There are quite a number of other overhead absorption (overhead recovery) rates which could have been used. A study of them is outside the scope of this book.

Stage 6
The overheads are then charged to products in one of two ways:

- if a job/product spends 8 machine hours in the machine department, it will be charged with 8 machine hours of overheads at the rate per machine hour;
- if a job/product spends 1½ direct labour hours in the paint department, it will be charged with 1½ direct labour hours' worth of overheads at the rate per direct labour hour.

As products move from department to department they *accumulate* a portion of each department's overheads. The overheads are being recovered hour by hour.

Stage 7
The administration, selling and distribution expenses are charged either to the profit and loss account or to jobs/products. The way in which they are treated is at the discretion of the management.

The following simplified, but comprehensive, example should help you to understand the process more fully.

Example 4.1 Van Chiu Ltd

We have been provided with the information shown in Tables 4.2 and 4.3 relating to Van Chiu Ltd, for their forthcoming period. The estimated number of direct labour hours in department F was 15,500 and the estimated number of machine hours in department G was 22,500.

1. Prepare a departmental overhead summary and calculate a direct labour hour rate for department F and a machine hour rate for department G.

Table 4.2 Van Chiu Ltd: estimated overhead expenditure

Estimated overhead expenses	£	Allocation or apportionment
Indirect materials and labour:		
Production department F	9,925	Allocation
Production department G	7,900	Allocation
Service department H	15,875	Allocation
Service department I	7,300	Allocation
Rent of buildings	24,000	Floor area
Insurance of buildings	3,000	Floor area
Supervision	28,000	Number of employees
Repairs and renewals	18,000	Technical estimate: F 30%, G 50%, H 10%, I 10%
Depreciation of machinery:		
Production department F	4,000	Allocation
Production department G	9,000	Allocation
Service department H	5,000	Allocation
Service department I	2,000	Allocation
	134,000	

Table 4.3 Van Chiu Ltd: apportionment data

	F	G	H	I
Area (in square metres)	250	600	100	50
Number of employees	17	10	3	2
Technical estimates for service departments				
The use of service H	60%	30%	–	10%
The use of service I	25%	75%	–	–

2. Prepare a quotation for a job, number WW658, to which the following data are applicable:
   (a) direct material: £394;
   (b) direct labour:
      department F: 6 hours at £8 per hour;
      department G: 2 hours at £9 per hour;
      machine hours in department G were 5.
   The company uses a mark-up of 30% on cost.

Answer

Having been provided with the predetermined overheads, we can prepare the departmental overhead summary in which we allocate and apportion the overheads to departments/cost centres. When this has been completed, we then share out the service department costs between user departments according to the technical estimates supplied. This will take us up to the point of having total overhead figures for departments F and G. See Table 4.4 for the overhead distribution summary.

We now know the total overhead which has been allocated and apportioned to production departments F and G, and the overhead absorption (recovery) rates for the two departments can now be calculated. The rate for production department F is:

Table 4.4 Van Chiu Ltd: overhead distribution summary

Overhead	Allocation or apportionment	Total £	Production departments		Service departments	
			F £	G £	H £	I £
Indirect materials and labour	Allocated	41,000	9,925	7,900	15,875	7,300
Rent and insurance	Floor area	27,000	6,750 (25%)	16,200 (60%)	2,700 (10%)	1,350 (5%)
Supervision	No. of employees	28,000 (17/32)	14,875 (10/32)	8,750 (3/32)	2,625 (2/32)	1,750
Repairs and renewals	Technical estimates	18,000	5,400 (30%)	9,000 (50%)	1,800 (10%)	1,800 (10%)
Depreciation	Allocated	20,000	4,000	9,000	5,000	2,000
		£134,000	40,950	50,850	28,000	14,200
Service H	Technical estimates		16,800 (60%)	8,400 (30%)	−28,000	2,800 (10%)
						17,000
Service I	Technical estimates		4,250 (25%)	12,750 (75%)	—	−17,000
		£134,000	£62,000	£72,000		

Table 4.5 Quotation for job WW658

		£
Direct materials		394
Direct labour	£	
(6 × £8) Department F	48	
(2 × £9) Department G	18	66
Overheads		
Department F 6 hrs @ £4	24	
Department G 5 hrs @ £3.20	16	40
Cost		500
add mark up @ 30% (profit)		150
		650

$$\frac{\text{overheads}}{\text{direct labour hours}} = \frac{£62,000}{15,500} = £4 \text{ per direct labour hour}$$

For production department G it is:

$$\frac{\text{overheads}}{\text{machine hours}} = \frac{£72,000}{22,500} = £3.20 \text{ per machine hour}$$

The quotation for the job WW658 can now be prepared, and is as shown in Table 4.5.

Comments

You should note that the quotation for the job WW658 is made up of four elements:

☐ Direct materials.
☐ Direct labour.
☐ Overheads.
☐ Mark-up/profit.

The direct materials and direct labour were given, but you should remember that they also will also have to be predetermined/estimated in practice.

Finally, note that for department G the hours used to arrive at the overhead cost of £16 were the 5 machine hours, *not* the direct labour hours. Why? Because the overheads for that department are being recovered using a machine hour rate.

Now see if you can solve a similar problem in order to firmly fix the overhead absorption process in your mind, before we take a look at the limitations of absorption costing.

Self-assessment Question 4.1

Throngfirth Manufacturing

Throngfirth Manufacturing operates three production departments: the machine department, paint department and assembly department, and two service departments:

stores and power. The budgeted overheads for the forthcoming period are as shown in Table 4.6.

They have also supplied you with the information given in Table 4.7, which should help you to apportion those overheads which cannot be allocated to departments.

From the data provided in Tables 4.6 and 4.7 you are required to:

1. Prepare a departmental overhead summary and calculate a machine hour rate for the machine department and direct labour hour rates for the other two production departments.

Table 4.6 Throngfirth Manufacturing: budgeted overheads

	£
Indirect materials and labour:	
Machine department	36,730
Paint department	11,270
Assembly department	11,900
Stores	16,680
Power	15,120
Other overheads:	
Fuel for power department	74,000
Building insurance	5,800
Lighting	3,800
Supervision	19,000
Machinery insurance	4,800
Canteen	24,200
Depreciation:	
Machine department	12,400
Paint department	6,300
Assembly department	2,100
Stores	1,400
Power	3,500
	249,000

Table 4.7 Throngfirth Manufacturing: apportionment data

	Machine department	Paint department	Assembly department	Stores	Power
Floor area (m^2)	8,000	2,000	4,000	1,000	1,000
Number of employees	6	2	8	2	2
Value of machinery (£000)	75	25	–	–	25
Direct labour hours	6,400	5,000	8,000		
Machine hours	20,000	–	–		
Stores usage (technical estimate)	25%	25%	40%	–	10%
Power usage (technical estimate)	60%	25%	15%	–	–

2. Calculate how much product PQ will cost if it takes £1,277 of raw materials and 15 hours of machine time in the machine department, and the following direct labour costs:
   (a) machine department: 4 hours @ £9 per hour;
   (b) paint department: 3 hours @ £8 per hour;
   (c) assembly: 16 hours @ £7 per hour.
3. Calculate the proposed selling price if a mark-up of 40% on cost is used.

The answers are to be found on pages 113–15.

The limitations of total absorption costing

The first limitation of absorption costing is the *accuracy of the predetermined overheads*. You should not lose sight of the fact that the overheads which are used are only estimates.

The selection of the bases of apportionment, e.g. floor area, number of employees, etc., depends upon the judgement of whoever has to make the selection. Different people could adopt differing bases of apportionment for the same type of expense, e.g. the rent of premises could be shared out according to floor area or cubic capacity.

There are many different methods which can be used for dealing with the distribution of service department costs to user departments. For example, the stores cost could be shared between user departments/cost centres according to the number of issue notes (material requisitions). However, although this may seem a reasonable and appropriate method, you should note that it does not take account of the value, weight or size of the materials.

Another problem arises because the *machine hours and/or the direct labour hours for the period also have to be estimated*.

Thus, when the actual figures become available the overheads may be more or less than those which were estimated for the period. This means that there will be either an *over- or under-absorption of overheads* charged to products. However, we cannot go back and rework the costs of the jobs/products; they are now history. The over- or under-absorption will have to be adjusted for in the profit and loss account.

You should also note that the treatment of administration, selling and distribution overheads, and research and development expenditure varies; they can be included in the job/product/service costs or charged direct to the profit and loss account as an expense.

It has been found that certain companies that did charge some of their research and development expenditure to products, tended to understate the profits earned by existing products and overstate the profits earned by newly introduced products. As a result they discontinued some of the existing products – products which were really more profitable than the new products!

An introduction to ABC (activity-based costing), an extension of the absorption costing method, will be covered in Chapter 5.

Summary: total absorption costing

Figure 4.1 sums up the essence of absorption costing. The overheads, i.e. indirect expenditure, both fixed and variable, have to be estimated, i.e. *predetermined* before the period to which they relate commences. Total absorption costing is also called **absorption costing**, **full costing** or **total costing**. It is just an attempt to ensure that all costs are covered. It does not profess to produce accurate job, product or service costs.

Overheads

Overhead/indirect cost is defined by CIMA (The Chartered Institute of Management Accountants) in the UK as 'Expenditure, labour, materials or services which cannot be economically identified with a specific saleable cost unit'. A cost unit could be a job, product or service.

Those overheads which can be identified and traced to a department or cost centre can be charged direct to the department or cost centre concerned, i.e. allocated. Those which cannot be identified or traced to a department or cost centre will have to be apportioned according to some arbitrary basis, e.g. floor area, number of employees, etc.

The costs of running the various service departments, such as stores and power, have to be accumulated to arrive at a cost for running each service. The service department cost is then shared out between user departments via technical estimates or some other arbitrary basis.

Overheads can be analysed into groups, e.g. production, administration, selling and distribution, research and development. They can also be subdivided into fixed overheads and variable overheads.

However, whatever the analysis or subdivision used, you should note that we are still dealing with *the same estimated overhead/indirect costs*.

Overhead absorption

In deciding which basis of apportionment (arbitrary basis) to use, the selector has to choose the method which is considered to be the most appropriate for the type of expense which has to be shared out between departments/cost centres.

Before the absorption rate can be calculated the machine hours and the direct labour hours have to be estimated for the forthcoming period. The absorption rates which we have used were selected because they reflect time, as a lot of overheads vary more with time than output. These rates were as follows:

$$\text{machine hour rate} = \frac{\text{machine department overheads}}{\text{number of machine hours for the department concerned}}$$

```
┌─────────────────────────────┐
│                             │
│       Direct material       │
│             +               │
│       Direct labour         │
│             +               │
│         Overhead            │
│             =               │
│     Job/product/service     │
│            cost             │
│                             │
└─────────────────────────────┘
```

Figure 4.2 Job/product/service cost

$$\text{direct labour hour rate} = \frac{\text{overheads for the department}}{\text{number of direct labour hours for the department concerned}}$$

Decisions have to be made about the treatment of administration, research and development, and selling and distribution overheads.

As jobs/products/services pass through a department/cost centre, they in effect 'clock up' a share of that particular department's/cost centre's overheads, e.g. at so much per machine hour or so much per direct labour hour. Thus, as a job/product/service goes from department to department it *accumulates a share of the firm's overheads*.

Note that a job/product/service cost is made up of the elements shown in Figure 4.2. Some businesses use this figure plus a mark-up to fix their selling price or their quotation for a job/product/service.

Services

Although the illustrations in this chapter relate to a manufacturing type of environment and internal services, those organizations which provide services, e.g. health, auditing, education, radio and television, etc. do face similar problems. They also have to cost their services and account for overheads, as illustrated in Figure 4.2.

Limitations

Finally, remember that absorption costing does have limitations, e.g. the accuracy of the forecast overheads, the accuracy of the estimated machine hours and direct labour hours, the selection of methods of apportionment, etc.

Further reading

Drury, C., *Costing: An Introduction*, International Thomson Business Press, 1998.
Hussey, J. and Hussey, R., *Cost and Management Accounting*, Macmillan, 1998.

5

Activity-based costing

Objectives

Having worked through the whole of this chapter, you should be able to:

☐ Describe and discuss briefly, the principal drawbacks of traditional total absorption costing.
☐ Define in your own words what is meant by:
  ● activity-based costing;
  ● cost objects;
  ● resource cost drivers;
  ● activity cost drivers;
  ● activity cost pools.

☐ Prepare profit statements using an activity-based costing approach.
☐ Appreciate the limitations of activity-based costing.

The drawbacks of total absorption costing which we reviewed in Chapter 4 provided an explanation of why it is not considered suitable for decision-making purposes. The principal drawbacks described in that chapter concerned:

☐ the problem of estimating the overheads;
☐ the judgements which have to be made in connection with the allocation and apportionment to departments/cost centres;
☐ the selection of the method by which service department costs are to be apportioned between user departments/cost centres;
☐ the estimation of the direct labour hours and/or machine hours for use in the calculation of the absorption (recovery) rate;
☐ the way in which administrative expenses, selling and distribution costs, etc., are to be dealt with;
☐ the under- or over-absorption of fixed overheads.

The principal objective of total absorption costing is to ensure that all the costs are recovered. There has always been a quest for something a little more sophisticated and something which could provide management with a little more help and assistance with their product/service costing/decision-making. Thus, in the late 1980s R. Cooper and R.S. Kaplan in the USA developed activity-based costing (ABC), a new, and more common-sense, approach for assigning overheads to products, services, jobs, distribution channels, sales areas, etc.

What is activity-based costing (ABC)?

A review of the definitions of activity-based costing and Figure 5.1 should provide you with a good insight into what activity-based costing is and how it works.

CIMA (Chartered Institute of Management Accountants) official terminology (1991) defines it as: 'Cost attribution to cost units on the basis of benefit received from indirect activities e.g. ordering, setting-up, assuring quality'.

It has also been defined as:

A process of using multiple cost drivers to predict and allocate costs to products and services; an accounting system collecting financial and operational data on the basis of the underlying nature and extent of business activities; an accounting information and costing system that identifies the various activities performed in an organization, collects costs on the basis of the underlying nature and extent of those activities, and assigns costs to products and services based on consumption of those activities by products and services. (Barfield *et al.*, 1993)

Burch (1994) describes it as: the collection of financial and non-financial data about an enterprise's activities for two primary purposes:

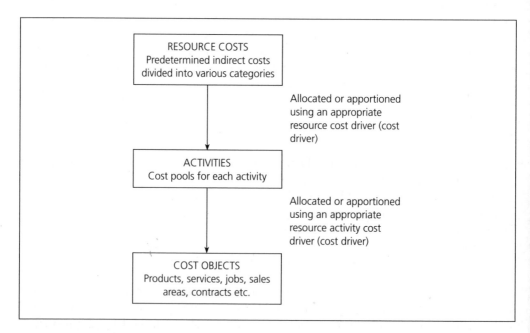

Figure 5.1 Activity-based costing

☐ Costing the enterprise's cost objectives, i.e. the products, services, batches, jobs, sales areas etc.
☐ Providing information for effective cost management through activity-based management.

Speaking at the European Accounting Conference which was held at Maastricht in April 1991, R.S. Kaplan said that he considered ABC to be much more than a product-costing system and that in his view it could be better described as a **resource consumption system**.

The resource costs

You need to appreciate at the outset that the costs which we are dealing with are the indirect costs, i.e. *the overheads*, as direct costs are charged direct to the cost object, e.g. the product or service. You should also note that the resource costs have still got to be estimated prior to the commencement of the budget period. The resource costs (indirect costs) could include costs such as insurance of buildings, wages and salaries, rent of premises, maintenance of equipment, depreciation of various fixed assets, etc.

The ones which are specific to one cost pool can be allocated to the cost pool concerned and do not present a problem. Those which are incurred on behalf of a number of cost pools will have to be apportioned using appropriate activity cost drivers (cost drivers). The resource cost driver (cost driver) is linked to the usage of the resource by the activity, for example in terms of:

■ the number of employees;
☐ the area in cubic capacity;
■ hours.

This type of cause-and-effect relationship is, as you may recall, used in total absorption costing. The principal difference here is that the cost centres are not production or service departments, but activities.

The activities

ABC is founded on the belief that the activities cause the costs and that the cost objects, e.g. products, services, etc., create the demand for those activities. The activities have to be identified and a cost pool (cost centre) established for each cost activity. There can be numerous activities. They can be allocated to a product/service where they are specific to that product/service. In cases where they serve a number of products/services they will have to be apportioned using activity cost drivers (cost drivers) as illustrated in Figure 5.2.

Thus, the amount assigned to each product/service will depend on the use made of the activity cost pool via an appropriate activity cost driver.

ACTIVITY COST POOL	ACTIVITY COST DRIVER (COST DRIVER)
Advertising	the value of sales in each sales area
Despatch	the number of despatch notes
Handling	the number of times which the material is handled
Inspection	the number of inspections
Purchasing	the number of purchase orders
Receiving (goods inwards)	the number of goods received notes
Setting-up	the number of set-ups
Stores	the number of stores issue notes

Figure 5.2 Assigning activity pool costs via activity (cost) drivers to cost objects

The ABC focus

ABC causes management to focus on what creates the demand for the resources and the redeployment or elimination of excess resources. ABC attempts to *estimate* the resources consumed by products.

Self-assessment Question 5.1

Having studied the definitions, and Figures 5.1 and 5.2, now see if you can answer the following recapitulation questions.

☐ Describe briefly the principal drawbacks which are associated with total absorption costing.

☐ Define activity-based costing in your own words.

☐ Which two primary purposes does activity-based costing attempt to serve?

☐ Give three examples of 'resource costs' and two examples of 'resource cost drivers'.

☐ Give three examples of 'activity cost pools' and two examples of 'activity cost drivers'.

☐ Which activity cost driver could be used for assigning costs to products/services, etc., for each of the following?

- advertising
- purchasing
- setting-up

On completion of this self-assessment, compare your answers with the appropriate sections of this chapter.

You should note that:

☐ resource cost drivers attempt to measure the resources consumed by the activity cost pools, and that

☐ activity cost drivers attempt to measure the activities consumed by the cost object, e.g. product, service, etc. The aim is to charge the cost object with the overheads which it actually uses.

The following step-by-step Example 5.1 should help you to understand the mechanics of an activity-based costing system.

Example 5.1

Lesaloke plc
The following indirect predetermined resource cost categories have been identified, together with the resource cost driver by which they will be assigned to activity cost pools, for the forthcoming period:

Resource Cost	£000	Resource Cost Driver
Wages and salaries	600	Number of employees
Computing	400	Computer hours
Office space	800	Cubic capacity

The activity cost pools and data relating to their consumption of the resource costs are:

Activity cost pool	Number of employees	Computer hours	Cubic capacity
Purchasing	5	40,000	6,000
Receiving	5	4,000	18,000
Despatch	10	6,000	24,000

The activity cost pools will therefore be:

	Purchasing £000	Receiving £000	Despatch £000	Total £000
Wages and salaries	150	150	300	600
Computing	320	32	48	400
Office space	100	300	400	800
	570	482	748	1,800

The resources have now been shared out between the 'activity cost pools' according to their estimated usage of the resource costs by each of the activities, by means of the resource cost drivers.

The company sells three products N, O and P and then assigns the costs of activities to them using the following activity cost drivers:

Activity cost pool	Activity cost driver the number of
Purchasing	purchase orders
Receiving	goods received notes
Despatch	despatch notes

The following estimates have been prepared for the period:

	Products			
Number of:	N	O	P	Total
Purchase orders	5,000	2,000	600	7,600
Goods received notes	6,000	3,000	640	9,640
Despatch notes	4,000	5,000	350	9,350

From the above information we can work out the cost per order/note for each of the activity cost drivers:

	Purchasing	Receiving	Despatch
Cost	£570,000	£482,000	£748,000
Activity cost driver	7,600 orders	9,640 notes	9,350 notes
Cost per order/note	**£75 per order**	**£50 per note**	**£80 per note**

We can now assign the activity pool costs to the three products, as follows:

	Products			
	N	O	P	Total
Purchasing @ £75 per order	375	150	45	570
Receiving @ £50 per note	300	150	32	482
Despatch @ £80 per note	320	400	28	748
Cost of overheads assigned to products	**995**	**700**	**105**	**1,800**

In this simplified example we only had three lots of resource costs, three activity cost pools and three products. In practice you will find that there are many more categories of resource costs, many more activity cost pools to deal with and many more products/services to contend with.

You should note that resource cost drivers and activity cost drivers can be:

☐ time-based;

☐ value-based (e.g. in £s sterling);

☐ transaction-based;

☐ percentage-based.

The one that should be used is the one which has a direct cause-and-effect relationship. Thus, with activity-based costing a choice has to be made as to which cost driver is the most appropriate for the assignment of resource costs to activities and activity costs to cost objects.

ABC – a brief but critical evaluation

ABC seeks to find out what causes the indirect expenditure (i.e. the overheads). This is not an easy task as many of the overheads vary more with time than with output and several of the suggested cost drivers are those which are already recommended for use in total absorption costing, e.g. the machine hours and the direct labour hours.

You need to note that the overheads that you are dealing with are the same overheads that you have to estimate and deal with for total absorption costing purposes. You also have to select which cost driver you consider to be the most appropriate, and this is not always clear-cut. In addition you have to estimate the number of machine hours, direct labour hours, set-ups, purchase orders, etc., before the period to which they relate commences.

Remember that when you deal with setting-up costs that the actual setting-up labour cost is a direct cost and should not be included in the overhead costs. For example, where a setter spends one hour setting up a machine for a production run for a batch of similar products, the setter's time can be charged to the specific batch concerned, i.e. it is a direct cost of the batch concerned.

One recommended way of sharing out the stores cost is to use the number of stores issue notes (stores requisitions) as the cost driver. This method does not take account of size, weight, value, handling problems, storage problems, etc. However, from this you should be able to observe and conclude that it would be impossible to find a way of sharing out this cost which could be described as both fair and accurate.

However, it is recognized that ABC is a step in the right direction, but not the end of the story, as the quest for something better continues to provoke thought, debate and research.

Self-assessment Question 5.2

The following self-assessment assumes that you would have no problem in assigning costs to resource cost pools. The mechanics for this are very similar to those which you came across earlier in the text when you allocated and apportioned overheads to cost centres.

Pawilkes & Co. Ltd

The company manufactures two products, D and E. The following budgeted information relating to the company for the forthcoming period has been made available to you:

	Products	
	D	**E**
Sales and production (000 units)	200	120
	£	£
Selling price (per unit)	12	28
Prime cost (per unit)	8	18
	Hours	Hours
Department 1 (machine hours per unit)	0.5	2
Department 2 (direct labour hours per unit)	0.25	3

Details of the amounts assigned to activity cost pools and their cost drivers are:

	Activity cost pool £000	Activity cost driver
Department 1	680	Machine hours
Department 2	410	Direct labour hours
Setting-up costs	40	No. of set-ups
Computing	200	No. of hours
Purchasing	100	No. of orders
	1,430	

You have also been provided with the following estimates for the period under review:

	Products		
	D	**E**	**Total**
	(000)	(000)	(000)
Machine hours	100	240	340
Direct labour hours	50	360	410
No. of set-ups	6	4	10
Computer (hours)	20	20	40
Purchasing (no. of orders)	40	10	50

Using an activity-based costing approach, prepare a profit statement which shows the profit or loss for each product and the total profit or loss.

When you have completed your attempt, compare it with the suggested solution which appears on page 115.

Summary: activity-based costing

Traditional total absorption costing is simply an attempt to ensure that all costs are re-covered. It does not produce product/service costs which can be described as fair and accurate and is therefore considered unsuitable for decision-making purposes.

The principal drawbacks associated with total absorption costing are:

- ☐ the predetermination of overheads, and
- ☐ their allocation and apportionment to cost centres;
- ☐ the estimation of figures such as machine hours and/or direct labour hours;
- ☐ decisions regarding the treatment of administration, selling and distribution expenses;
- ☐ the under- or over-absorption of fixed overheads.

ABC (activity-based costing)

Activity-based costing attempts to identify which of the activities cause the overhead costs and then link them up via the use of **cost drivers** (i.e. resource cost drivers and activity cost drivers) to **cost objects** such as products, services, sales areas, etc. The cost objects in effect create the demand for the activities. (See Figure 5.1 for a further review of how activity-based costing systems work.) For examples of activity cost pools and activity cost drivers see Figure 5.2.

For activity-based costing to have a chance of working, it is necessary to:

- ☐ identify the activities;
- ☐ create cost pools for each resource centre and each activity;
- ☐ identify the cost drivers for resource cost drivers and activity cost drivers;
- ☐ assign costs to cost objects, e.g. products, services, etc.

It is accepted that ABC is a more accurate method for dealing with overheads compared to total absorption costing, and a step in the right direction. However, quite a number of the recommended cost drivers are just the same as they are for total absorption costing, e.g. using the number of direct labour hours or the number of stores issue notes, and therefore suffer from the same limitations, problems and drawbacks.

Costs do not cause activities – activities cause costs.

Further reading and references

Atrill, P. and McLaney, E., *Management Accounting for Non-specialists*, Prentice Hall Europe, 1998.

Barfield, J.T., Raiborn, C.A. and Kinney, M.R., *Cost Accounting Traditions and Innovations*, West Publishing, 1993.

Burch, J.G., *Cost and Management Accounting: A Modern Approach*, West Publishing, 1994.

Drury, J.C., *Management and Cost Accounting*, International Thomson Business Press, 2000.

Horngren, C.T., Foster, G. and Srikant, M.D., *Cost Accounting, A Managerial Emphasis*, Prentice Hall, 2000.

6

Marginal costing and breakeven analysis

Objectives

When you have completed your study of this chapter you should:

☐ Know how marginal costing differs from absorption costing.
☐ Understand the relationship between selling price, variable cost and the contribution.
☐ Be able to calculate the contribution and profit volume ratio and use them to calculate the breakeven point.
☐ Be able to solve problems involving profit targets and limiting factors.
☐ Understand and be able to prepare an elementary breakeven chart.
☐ Appreciate the limitations and drawbacks of marginal costing and breakeven analysis.

Marginal costing

Marginal costing (which is also known as **variable costing** or **direct costing** or **differential costing**) is concerned with the treatment of fixed costs and the relationship which exists between three figures: sales, variable cost and the contribution.

What is the contribution? The **contribution** is the name given to the difference between sales and variable cost in the marginal cost equation.

Example 6.1 Contribution and profit

A product sells at £50 and has a variable cost of £30, and during the period ended 30 June 20X0 2,000 units were sold. Fixed costs for that period amounted to £25,000. The contribution and profit would be calculated as shown in Table 6.1.

It can be observed from Example 6.1 that the *contribution contributes towards the recovery of the fixed costs and profit*. Marginal costing is a technique which can be used as part of the decision-making process to show the effect of changes/possible changes in demand and/or selling prices and/or variable costs. It can, for example, be used: to identify the most

Table 6.1 Marginal costing relationships

		per unit (£)	2,000 units (£)	% of sales
	Selling price	50	100,000	100
less	Variable costs	30	60,000	60
	Contribution	20	40,000	40
less	Fixed costs (overheads)		25,000	
	Profit		15,000	

Table 6.2 A multi-product environment

£000	Products A	B	C	D	Total £
Contribution	20	34	36	20	110
less Fixed costs					78
Profit					32

profitable projects, in make-or-buy decisions, or in deciding whether or not to enter into a special contract. Variable costs include only those costs which can be identified with and traced to products (or services), e.g. direct labour, direct materials, direct expenses and variable overheads. The fixed costs (overheads) are those which cannot be identified with and traced to the products (or services). They tend to vary more with time than output, and are treated as **period costs**. This means that the fixed costs are not included in product (service) costs. They are simply written off, in total, against the total contribution(s) generated from the sale of all the firm's products (services), for the period in which they were incurred: see Table 6.2. This treatment of fixed costs also means that because they are not included in product costs they are *not carried forward into the future as part of the valuation of the stocks of work in progress and finished goods.*

The profit volume ratio (PV ratio)

The profit volume ratio explains the relationship between the contribution and sales and is calculated as follows:

$$\frac{\text{contribution}}{\text{sales}} \times 100 \quad \text{or} \quad \frac{\text{contribution per unit}}{\text{selling price per unit}} \times 100$$

Using the figures in Table 6.1 this works out as:

$$\frac{£40,000}{£100,000} \times 100 = 40\%$$

You may have observed that this has already been shown in Table 6.1. It is simply the contribution expressed as a percentage of sales. We now have enough information to calculate the **breakeven point**, *the point at which sales revenue and costs are equal,* or the point at which the contribution generated is equal to the fixed costs:

$$\frac{\text{fixed costs}}{\text{contribution per unit}} = \text{breakeven point in units}$$

$$\frac{£25,000}{£20} = 1,250 \text{ units}$$

To convert this to the breakeven point in terms of value, we just multiply the 1,250 units by the unit selling price of £50:

1,250 units × £50 = £62,500

Or we could calculate the breakeven point using the profit volume ratio, as follows:

$$\text{Fixed cost} \div \text{PV ratio} = £25,000 \times \frac{100}{40} = £62,500$$

The contribution table

A good way of dealing with problems involving changes in selling prices and/or variable costs is to construct a contribution table (see Table 6.4). The table shows the effect of the change or changes on the contribution.

Example 6.2 The effect of a change on the contribution

Using the figures from Table 6.3 as our starting point, we can work out the effects of different strategies for the forthcoming period (see Table 6.4).

It can be seen that Strategy 2 will generate the highest profit in the forthcoming period, provided the forecast demand materializes.

Table 6.3 Strategic alternatives

	Selling price per unit £	Variable cost per unit £	Demand (units)	Fixed costs £
Current period	50	30	2,000	25,000
Strategy 1	Increase by £5	No change	1,800	28,000
Strategy 2	No change	Reduce by £3	2,500	35,000
Strategy 3	No change	Increase by £2	2,200	28,000

Table 6.4 Contribution table

		Current period	1	2	3
		£	£	£	£
	Selling price (per unit)	50	55	50	50
less	Variable cost (per unit)	30	30	27	32
	Contribution (per unit)	20	25	23	18
	Units sold (demand)	2,000	1,800	2,500	2,200
	Total contribution	40,000	45,000	57,500	39,600
less	Fixed costs	25,000	28,000	35,000	28,000
	Profit	15,000	17,000	22,500	11,600

It should be apparent, from a study of Example 6.2, that a movement in either the selling price or variable cost will be reflected by a movement in the contribution, as follows:

☐ An increase in the selling price or a decrease in the variable cost will result in an increase in the contribution.
☐ Vice versa, a decrease in the selling price or an increase in the variable cost will bring about a decrease in the contribution.

Note also that the fixed costs may vary, e.g. if the decision is taken to purchase a new machine, the fixed machine cost will increase.

Profit targets

If management sets a profit target, all you have to do is remember that the contribution is equal to the *fixed costs plus the profit target* (see Figure 6.1). Adding the fixed costs which have to be covered to the profit target will give you the total contribution which needs to be generated. The total contribution required must then be divided by the contribution per unit. This tells you how many units will have to be sold in order to generate the required contribution:

$$\frac{\text{contribution required}}{\text{contribution per unit}} = \text{the number of units which must be sold in order to generate the contribution required}$$

Fixed costs
plus Profits or *less* Loss
=
Contribution required

Figure 6.1 The contribution required

Example 6.3 Generating the required contribution

Using the current period information in Table 6.4, and assuming management has set a target profit of £24,000, we can work out how many units we would have to sell to achieve this (see Table 6.5).

Table 6.5 Dealing with profit targets

	£
Fixed costs	25,000
add profit target	24,000
Contribution required	49,000

$$\therefore \text{ must sell } \frac{£49,000}{£20} = 2,450 \text{ units}$$

In terms of value, this would be
2,450 units @ £50 unit selling price = £122,500

Self-assessment Question 6.1

Now attempt the following self-assessment question. When you have completed it, compare your answer with the suggested solution on pages 116–18.

Heaton Postex plc

Heaton Postex plc manufactures CD players and has provided you with the following information on variable costs per unit for the current year, 20X8.

Direct labour:	£20
Direct materials:	£64
Variable overheads:	£12
Total variable costs:	£96

Fixed costs: £164,000.
Selling price per unit: £120.
Expected sales: 40,000 units.

The sales target for next year, 20X9, has been set at 50,000 units, and fixed costs are expected to rise to £186,000. The selling price would rise to £125 per unit and the total variable costs would increase by £4 per unit.
Calculate the following:

1. The total contribution and net profit for 20X8 and 20X9.
2. The breakeven point for 20X8 and 20X9.
3. The sales level which would have to be attained in 20X9 in order to generate a profit equal to that which was earned in 20X8.
4. The maximum amount which could be spent on additional fixed costs at a sales level of 56,000 units to produce a profit of £1,200,000.

Table 6.6 Limiting factors: material supply

	Product P	Product Q
Selling price (per unit)	800	500
Variable cost (per unit)	500	300
Material required to produce one unit	4 litres	2 litres

Limiting factors

The limiting factor (also called the **key factor** or **principal budget factor**) is the factor which constrains/limits the activities of a business. Thus, when budgets are being prepared, the limiting factor is the starting point of the budgeting process and has to be taken into account first. For example, if sales demand were the limiting factor, i.e. if the company could only sell a limited number of products during a period, this would limit the production needed, the amount of labour, the material requirements, and so on. It is not a sound business policy to produce more than you can sell!

Other examples of limiting factors are as follows:

☐ The supply of materials, e.g. Table 6.6.
☐ The availability of labour.
☐ Production capacity.
☐ Finance.
☐ Legislation.

However, limiting factors are not static. Management can, by its actions, eliminate them altogether or reduce their effect.

What can management do where the supply of certain materials is limited?
Answer: lots. Management can search for new supplies; investigate the use of a substitute; have the product redesigned to use none or less of the material concerned; improve production and inspection techniques to reduce waste and the number of defectives.

What can be done if there is a shortage of labour?
Answer: quite a lot. Where labour is the limiting factor management can bring workers in from other areas; attract labour from other countries; introduce overtime and shift work; undertake to train or organize the training of new operatives; lease or buy labour-saving machines/robots; use subcontractors.

What can management do if there is insufficient production capacity?
Answer: again, quite a lot. Managers can introduce more overtime and shift work; lease or buy more machinery/robots; use subcontractors; reorganize the production flow to reduce idle/non-productive time; review the design of the product, e.g. the degree of precision needed, etc., so as to reduce the time spent making the product.

Can management do anything if finance is in short supply?

Answer: yes, finance is always available from a multitude of sources, but usually at a cost which reflects the risk to the lender! In addition to loans from various sources there are also government schemes/grants; EU schemes/grants; sale and lease back; the sale of the company's own surplus fixed assets, e.g. buildings, machines, equipment and current assets such as stocks of raw materials, fuels and finished goods; the issue of share capital, etc.

What can be done if the limiting factor is legislation?

Answer: not a lot. However, management can approach local council representatives, MPs, trade associations, chambers of trade and pressure groups.

When a business's activities are constrained because of a limiting factor, it has to attempt to maximize its contribution. This can be done by means of a simple technique. The technique calculates *the contribution per unit of the limiting factor*. The course of action which gives the highest contribution per unit of the limiting factor, e.g. per hour or per kilo, is the one which will maximize the contribution.

Example 6.4 Maximizing the contribution

The supply of a particular material is limited to 5,000 litres per period. It can be used to produce either product P or product Q, details of which are given in Table 6.6.

The contribution per unit of the limiting factor, i.e. the contribution per litre, would be calculated as shown in Table 6.7.

The maximum contribution possible is therefore:

quantity of material available × contribution per litre

Product P 5,000 litres × £75 = £375,000
Product Q 5,000 litres × £100 = £500,000

Product Q is therefore the one which should be produced. By producing it, a contribution of £500,000 is generated, £125,000 greater than the contribution which could be generated by producing product P.

Table 6.7 Contribution per litre

		Product P £	product Q £
	Selling price (per unit)	800	500
less	Variable cost (per unit)	500	300
	Contribution	300	200
	$\dfrac{\text{contribution}}{\text{quantity needed}}$	$\dfrac{£300}{4} = £75/\text{litre}$	$\dfrac{£200}{2} = £100/\text{litre}$

Table 6.8 Scoubado Manufacturing: product information

	Product J £	K £	L £
Selling price (per unit)	75	108	59
Cost per unit			
Direct material	30	64	20
Direct labour	6	9	4
Variable overhead	14	11	15
	50	84	39
Time taken to produce one unit	30 min	45 min	20 min

Self-assessment Question 6.2

Now see if you can solve the following limiting factor problem; the figures do change and are more complex, but the principles/techniques remain unchanged.

Scoubado Manufacturing

Scoubado Manufacturing make three products – J, K and L. Details are given in Table 6.8.

The constraint under which the company is currently working is that, until management can take appropriate action, its *productive hours are limited to 42 hours per day.* However, all sales of J in excess of 30 units will have to be sold at £72 per unit; all sales of K in excess of 24 units will have to be sold at £105 per unit; and all sales of L in excess of 60 units will have to be sold at £49 per unit.

Work out the maximum contribution which could be earned per day. (For the suggested answer please turn to pages 118–19 *but only* after you have attempted to solve the problem yourself.)

The limitations and drawbacks of marginal costing

It will always be difficult to assess how both fixed costs and variable costs will be affected by changes in output. Direct labour, direct materials and variable expenses can be affected in a multitude of ways. It must be pointed out here that one of the drawbacks, which is frequently not appreciated, is that it is not always such an easy task to segregate costs into their fixed and variable elements. Some items of expenditure which are very similar can be treated differently, e.g. the rent of machinery paid on a fixed rental would be treated as a fixed cost, but if the rental paid was based on output it would be treated as a variable cost! Direct labour paid at a fixed amount irrespective of the level of output would be a fixed cost!

Oversimplified marginal costing can lead to the underpricing of products and a loss-making situation. The incorrect assumption made by certain users that fixed costs tend to remain constant, irrespective of the level of activity, may account for the underpricing of certain products and loss-making situations.

Breakeven analysis

In Chapter 1 you were introduced to cost behaviour. However, a quick recap may prove helpful.

☐ *Fixed costs*
   Those costs which, in the short term, remain unchanged within a relevant range of activity (see Figure 6.2).

☐ *Variable costs*
   Those costs which, in the short term, vary directly with the level of activity (output) within a relevant range (see Figure 6.3).

A combination of the two is known as a semi-variable or a semi-fixed cost, e.g. a cost which is made up of a fixed rental plus an amount which is paid per unit of output produced.

At the outset you should note that breakeven analysis is a short-term planning device and should not be used in isolation but in conjunction with other data/information. Note that in the short term fixed and variable costs will only remain constant within a relevant range of output/level of activity.

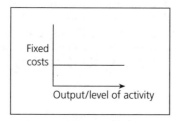

Figure 6.2 Fixed costs

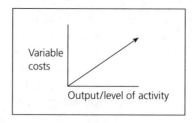

Figure 6.3 Variable costs

The traditional breakeven chart (graph)

Example 6.5 Constructing a breakeven chart

We will now construct a breakeven chart using the following information:

Output: 125,000 units
Sales: £500,000
Variable cost: £250,000
Fixed cost: £100,000

We first draw up our chart and then insert the sales line (see Figure 6.4).

Next we draw the fixed-cost line which runs parallel to the base of the chart (i.e. the output) (see Figure 6.5).

Finally, we include the variable costs by adding them on to the fixed costs. This line is drawn from £100,000 at 0 output to £350,000 at 125,000 output. This line is the total-cost line, i.e. fixed cost £100,000 plus variable cost £250,000 = £350,000 total cost (see Figure 6.6).

Having completed our breakeven chart (Figure 6.6) we can read off the breakeven point at £200,000 sales and costs and 50,000 output, the point at which costs and revenue (sales/income) are equal, i.e. where the sales line crosses the total cost line, or the point at which the contribution generated is equal to the fixed costs.

For proof see Table 6.9.

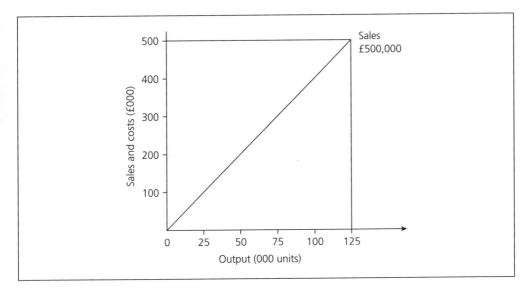

Figure 6.4 Sales

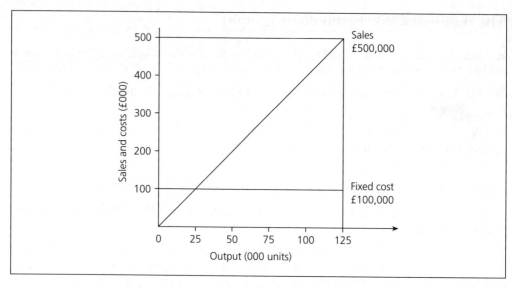

Figure 6.5 Sales and fixed costs

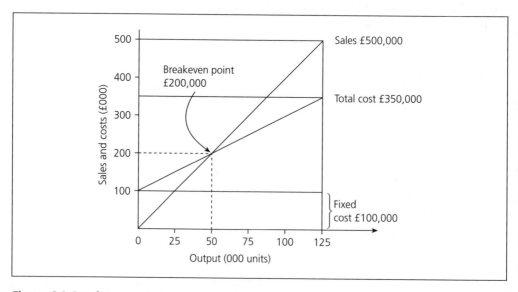

Figure 6.6 Breakeven point

Table 6.9 Calculating the breakeven point

	Per unit £	125,000 units £000	
Sales	4	500	
less Variable cost	2	250	
Contribution	2	250	(50% profit volume ratio)
less Fixed cost		100	
Profit		150	

Breakeven point = fixed cost ÷ PV ratio = £100,000 × $\dfrac{100}{50}$ = £200,000

or

$= \dfrac{\text{fixed cost}}{\text{contribution per unit}} = \dfrac{£100,000}{£2} = 50,000$ units

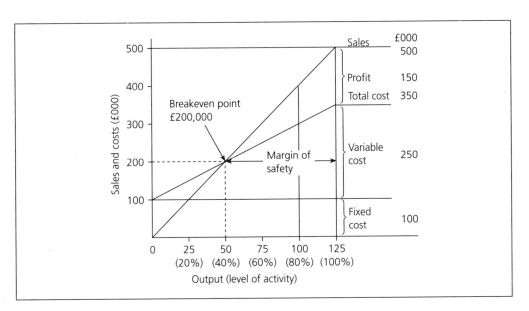

Figure 6.7 Conventional breakeven chart

Now let us take a closer look at the chart which we have just completed, and see what else it can tell us (Figure 6.7).

☐ The logic of the calculations involved can be followed as per the right-hand side of the chart, i.e. sales £500,000 less total cost £350,000 = profit £150,000, total cost £350,000 = variable cost £250,000 + fixed cost £100,000.

☐ Above the breakeven point we make a profit, below it we make a loss.

☐ The margin of safety is the difference between the breakeven point and the selected output/level of activity. This indicates the extent to which the level of activity must fall before a loss-making situation is reached, and vice versa.

Table 6.10 A profit proof: using marginal costing

		£000
	Contribution from 100,000 units @ £2 per unit	200
less	Fixed cost	100
	Profit	100

☐ The horizontal base line of the chart can be expressed in terms of either output or level of activity.

☐ By projecting a vertical line from the base line, e.g. at 100,000 units output (80% level of activity) we can use the chart to read off the fixed cost, total cost and sales applicable to this particular level of activity. You can see that the vertical line drawn from 100,000 units output (80% level of activity) cuts the fixed-cost line at £100,000, the total-cost line at £300,000 and the sales line at £400,000. The gap between sales and total cost of £100,000 represents the profit which should be achieved at the 80% level of activity: see Table 6.10 for proof.

The contribution breakeven chart (graph)

The contribution breakeven chart is an alternative way of showing the information which we used to construct our traditional breakeven chart. Using the same information as Example 6.5 we will look at its construction in two phases. First, we draw up the chart and then insert the sales line and the variable-cost line, both of which are drawn from the base line point 0 (see Figure 6.8).

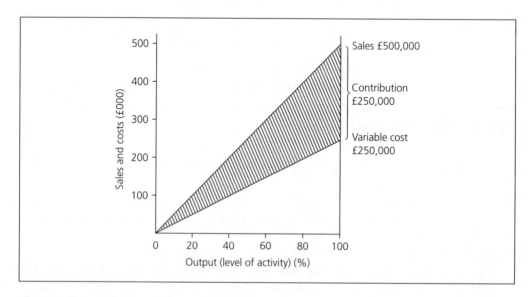

Figure 6.8 Contribution, sales and variable cost

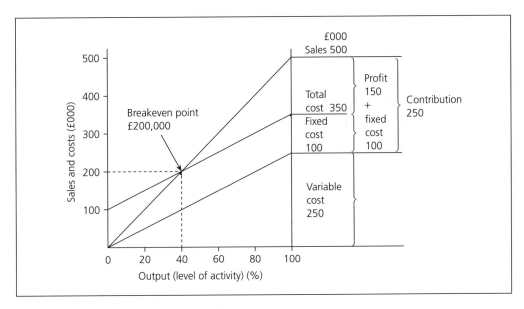

Figure 6.9 Contribution breakeven chart

This incomplete breakeven chart (Figure 6.8) illustrates that sales of £500,000 less variable cost £250,000 = contribution £250,000. The principal advantage of this chart is that it shows, very clearly, the contribution which is being generated at different levels of activity.

The fixed costs of £100,000 are then added to the variable costs and the total-cost line drawn from £100,000 at 0% level of activity to £350,000 at 100% level of activity; the fixed costs are plotted parallel to the variable costs (see Figure 6.9).

☐ Figure 6.9 shows that below the breakeven point the fixed costs are not being covered. When the contribution generated has covered fixed costs, the remainder is profit.
☐ The final contribution breakeven chart (Figure 6.9) illustrates that the contribution £250,000 less fixed cost £100,000 = profit £150,000.

The profit graph/profit volume diagram

This is an alternative type of breakeven chart and should help you to understand the profit volume ratio more clearly. To draw it you need to know any two of the three figures: fixed cost, profit and breakeven point. Again, using the same figures as in Example 6.5, the graph would be as shown in Figure 6.10.

☐ The line which joins the fixed costs to the profit is, in fact, the contribution line, i.e. it represents fixed costs £100,000 + profit £150,000 = £250,000 contribution.
☐ The breakeven point is again £200,000.

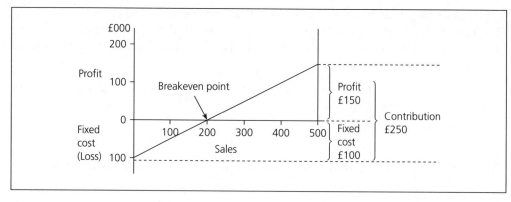

Figure 6.10 Profit graph/profit volume diagram

Self-assessment Question 6.3

Now it's your turn. May I suggest that you find some graph paper and then attempt the following problem. When you have completed your answer, compare it with the suggested answer on pages 119–20.

Holme Honley Products plc

The firm's forecast figures for the forthcoming period are as shown in Table 6.11.

1. Prepare a breakeven chart and show the breakeven point and margin of safety.
2. Show what the position would be if the output achieved was only 15,000 units (i.e. a 60 per cent level of activity).

Table 6.11 Holme Honley Products plc forecast figures

Output (units)	25,000
	per unit
Sales	£100·
Variable cost	£40
Fixed costs	£1,200,000

The limitations and drawbacks of breakeven analysis

The assumptions upon which breakeven analysis is based, e.g. how costs behave, a constant product mix, constant selling prices, etc., do not always hold true in the real world, even in the short term.

☐ Fixed and variable costs will not always behave as expected.
☐ Sales of a product may have to be made to different customers/market segments at different prices.

☐ The decisions made by management can affect variable and fixed costs.
☐ Efficiency levels within a manufacturing concern are not always constant.
☐ The product mix will have to respond to changes in demand and cannot therefore be forecast with accuracy.

Remember also that the breakeven chart is most useful if used in the short term and in conjunction with other data.

Summary: marginal costing and breakeven analysis

Marginal costing

Marginal costing differs from absorption costing because of the way in which it deals with fixed costs (overheads):

☐ Fixed costs, in marginal costing, are treated as **period costs**, i.e. they are written off in the period in which they are incurred.
☐ Fixed costs are not included in stock valuations and are not therefore carried forward to future accounting periods.

The marginal cost equation expresses what marginal costing is all about (see Figure 6.11). It is about the relationship between sales, variable cost and the contribution. Movements in the selling price and/or variable cost will be reflected by a corresponding movement in the contribution. If the selling price goes up or the variable cost goes down, the contribution will go up by the same amount and vice versa. The contribution generated contributes towards the recovery of fixed costs, the remainder being the profit. The contribution per unit can be very useful when it comes to solving problems such as the following:

How many units must be sold in order to break even?

$$\frac{\text{fixed costs}}{\text{contribution per unit}} = \text{breakeven point in units}$$

How many units must be sold to produce a specified profit target?

$$\frac{\text{fixed cost} + \text{profit target}}{\text{contribution per unit}} = \text{no. of units which must be sold to achieve the profit target}$$

```
        Sales
         less
     Variable cost
          =
     Contribution
```

Figure 6.11 Marginal cost equation

Note that, when dealing with profit target problems, the key is to calculate the total contribution which must be generated:

total contribution required = fixed cost + profit target.

The **profit volume ratio** explains the relationship between the contribution and sales:

$$\text{PV ratio} = \frac{\text{contribution}}{\text{sales}} \times 100 \qquad \text{or} \quad \frac{\text{contribution per unit}}{\text{selling price per unit}} \times 100$$

This can also be used to help solve problems, e.g. to compute the breakeven point in terms of value:

breakeven point = fixed costs ÷ PV ratio

If a constraint, e.g. the supply of materials, productive hours available, etc., limits the activities of a business, there is a **limiting factor** (**key factor** or **principal budget factor**) at work and a simple technique can be applied in order to solve the problems which emerge. The technique expresses the *contribution per unit of the limiting factor*, e.g. contribution per kilo, contribution per litre, contribution per hour, etc. Where a choice has to be made between alternative products, the products which give the highest contribution per unit of the limiting factor should be produced, as this will maximize the contribution.

The impact of a limiting factor can be eliminated/reduced by the actions of management.

Marginal costing, which is also called 'direct costing' or 'variable costing' or 'differential costing', is certainly a very useful decision-making technique. However, it must be appreciated that its use can lead to underpricing and that it is not always as easy as might be imagined to separate the fixed from variable costs.

Breakeven analysis

The construction of a breakeven chart is a relatively straightforward activity. The breakeven point can be computed mathematically, so why produce a chart? The answer lies in the fact that with the chart you can read off the position at various levels of output/ activity and highlight the margin of safety. The limitations of breakeven analysis stem from the fact that in practice costs do not always behave as might be expected: sales of a product may have to be made using a variety of prices and the product mix is difficult to forecast.

Further reading

Atrill, P. and McLaney, E., *Management Accounting for Non-specialists*, Prentice Hall Europe, 1998.
Drury, C., *Management Accounting for Business Decisions*, International Thomson Business Press, 1997.
Upchurch, A., *Management Accounting*, Prentice Hall Europe, 1998.

7

Budgeting and budgetary control

Objectives

When you have reached the end of this chapter, you should:

☐ Know the principles of effective budgeting.
☐ Be able to explain the following terms:
  ● a budget;
  ● budgetary control;
  ● the principal budget factor;
  ● control by responsibility;
  ● management by exception.
☐ Know why it is important to prepare a cash budget (cash flow forecast).
☐ Be able to prepare a cash budget, budgeted profit and loss account and a budgeted balance sheet.
☐ Be able to identify the differences between a cash budget and a budgeted profit and loss account, and also to appreciate why the increase/decrease in the cash balance is different from the profit (loss) for a period.
☐ Appreciate that budgets are interrelated.
☐ Understand how flexible budgets are constructed and why it is important to use them.
☐ Be familiar with the behavioural aspects of budgeting.
☐ Know how zero base budgeting (ZBB) works.

We will now take a look at the household budget and see how the principles followed there apply (even more so) to both public- and private-sector organizations.

Introduction: the household budget

The family depicted in our diagram (Figure 7.1) will have to do as follows:

☐ Work in harmony.
☐ Adopt a common-sense approach.
☐ Set targets which are realistic and attainable.
☐ Decide upon the allocation of their scarce resources.

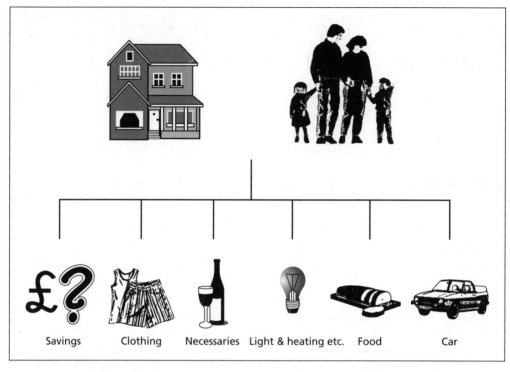

Figure 7.1 The household budget

☐ Consider trade-offs, i.e. all of the various alternatives.
☐ Appreciate the interrelationships between the various budgets.
☐ Hold meetings to discuss targets etc.
☐ Set objectives.
☐ Formulate policy.
☐ Participate in setting budgets.
☐ Cooperate, coordinate and communicate effectively.
☐ Prepare in advance of the budget period.
☐ Work to a budget preparation timetable.
☐ Identify the principal budget factor (i.e. limiting factor or key factor).
☐ Prepare flexible budgets.
☐ Delegate responsibility.
☐ Monitor progress.
☐ Take corrective action.
☐ Ensure that behavioural factors are taken into account.
☐ Make assumptions about the future.
☐ Revise the budgets to take account of changes in the assumptions which were made, e.g. changes in the business environment.

Quite a list; but also a good indication of exactly what effective budgeting and budgetary control entails.

Principles

Having listed the principles we will now look at them in a little more depth. Managers/executives responsible for the budgeting process will need to:

☐ Work together in *harmony* and *adopt a common-sense approach* throughout the budgeting process. This will involve the realistic appraisal of income and expenditure and the employment of capital.

☐ *Set attainable targets.* A budget which includes unattainable targets is most likely to be rejected by the people involved. From a management point of view, it is most important that budgets are accepted as being fair and reasonable.

☐ Decide upon how they are going to *share out the scarce resources* which they have at their disposal between the competing factions, e.g. alternative projects, production needs v. research and development needs v. marketing needs, and so on. This will involve discussions, negotiations, inter-personal skills and trade-offs.

☐ Appreciate the fact that *budgets are interrelated*, e.g. there is a link between the income budget and the expenditure budget. If income is to be used for one particular type of expenditure then it is not available to finance other expenditure. (See budget relationships and Figure 7.3 later in this chapter.)

☐ Attend meetings to discuss the setting of **objectives**, and the formulation of the **policy**, which they must follow in order to achieve the objectives. Many organizations do in fact have a budget committee which consists of representatives from all of the functional areas, e.g. production, marketing, finance, research and development, administration, selling and distribution, etc., and *a budget controller*, i.e. a person who oversees and coordinates their activities. The budget controller will seek to ensure that relevant information/data are collected, analysed, collated and distributed, to assist those who need it for their budget preparation. He/she must also attempt to secure the cooperation of others and to see that committee decisions are communicated clearly and effectively.

☐ Ensure that all those who should be involved get a chance to *participate in the budget preparation process*. Participation/involvement by, e.g., certain worker-representatives and/or supervisors can result in the setting of more realistic budgets and improved morale/motivation. The people involved may even bring to the attention of management, information which is vital to the success of the budgeting process.

☐ Hold their meetings well before the new budget period commences. They will have to devote time to the discussion of plans, the review of data and the revision of plans, etc. Hence the need for a *timetable for the budget preparation period*, so that by the time the new budget period commences, the budget is ready to be implemented. This preparation of budgets in advance is a prerequisite for effective budgeting.

	Simple Budget and Actual Comparative Statement (Details of purpose, etc.) Date			
Item	Actual £000	Budget £000	Variance £000	Reasons for variance

Figure 7.2 Simple budget and actual comparative statement (*details for the previous year could also be included for comparison*).

☐ From the outset, *identify their principal budget factor* (*limiting factor, key factor*), e.g. demand, as this will constrain their activities (see also limiting factors in marginal costing in Chapter 6). They will also have to decide whether or not to take action designed to eliminate or reduce the effects of the principal budget factor.

☐ *Plan for changes* in the basic assumptions upon which the budgets were based. This is why budgets should, where possible, be flexible, i.e. designed to change as levels of activity (output) change, and be revised to take account of environmental change.

☐ *Delegate the authority/responsibility* for a specific part of the budget to a particular person. This is known as '*control by responsibility*'. The person concerned will have to attempt, for example, to keep their spending in line with the targets set and provide explanations for periods in which targets are exceeded.

☐ *Monitor progress* at frequent intervals, e.g. monthly, by looking at budget and actual comparative statements, drafted along the lines of Figure 7.2.

Just like the householder, company/organization managers/executives will be particularly interested in significant adverse variances. These would be highlighted on the above type of statement/report (Figure 7.2), together with the reasons why they occurred. Managers can then devote their time and energy into putting right whatever is going wrong.

To focus on these reported significant adverse variances is known as *management by exception*. This should ensure the early detection of items which are not going according to plan. *Early detection means early action!*

☐ Appreciate that *budgets do affect people's behaviour* and that behavioural factors cannot and should not be ignored.

The variance is the difference between the actual and the budget. For example, if the actual expenditure exceeds the budgeted expenditure, it is adverse, i.e. an overspend. If the actual expenditure falls short, it is a favourable variance.

Self-assessment Question 7.1

Budgetary control self-check

From what you have read in this chapter so far, see if you can define, in your own words, the following key terms:

- A budget.
- Budgetary control.
- The principal budget factor.
- Control by responsibility.
- Management by exception.

When you have attempted to answer this self-assessment question, please turn to pages 121–2 and compare your answer with that suggested.

Practical considerations

Having established the principles of budgeting and budgetary control, we will conclude this section of the chapter by pointing out a number of practical considerations.

First, there needs to be an acceptance throughout the company/organization that budgeting is *a management planning technique* and that its use can greatly improve efficiency. Yes, budgeting/budgetary control should help the company/organization to compete in the market place and promote its long-term survival. Managers should therefore show by their actions that they *accept and approve of the budget*. Their *acceptance/approval* should be very clearly communicated to all those concerned. They should ensure that all of the personnel involved in the budgeting process are *educated* as to its benefits/principles and the way in which it operates within the company/organization.

A minor point, worthy of note, is that the actual and budgeted figures must match as regards content, i.e. they must be computed in the same way.

Finally, control should really be directed towards problem solving, constructive comments and the taking of corrective action by management, rather than recrimination.

Budget relationships

The budgeting process is rather like a large jigsaw, i.e. all the pieces must fit together, in order to form a coherent picture (see Figure 7.3). Budgets are interrelated. Something which affects one budget will tend to have a ripple effect in that it will also affect other budgets. Thus, during the budget preparation period the budget committee has to meet regularly to ensure that the individual functional budgets, e.g. sales, production, plant utilization, etc., all fit together. Examples 7.1 and 7.2 illustrate how the production budget would be arrived at, and the close link with the sales budget.

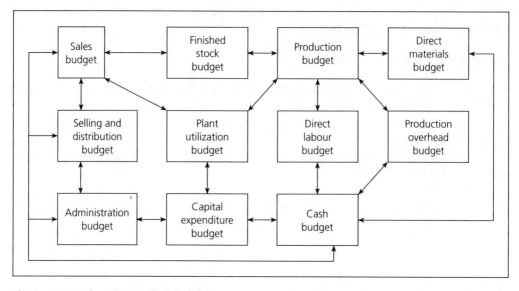

Figure 7.3 Budget interrelationships

Example 7.1 The calculation of budgeted production

Data relating to the forthcoming budget period are shown in Table 7.1.

The production budget would be as in Table 7.2.

The 12,700 units could be produced provided the company/organization had sufficient plant capacity, could organize an adequate supply of direct materials and direct labour, and had enough finance available. Thus, if the sales budget, which in the absence of a principal budget factor is the most usual starting point, is increased, the production budget will also have to be increased, as will the direct material budget and so on.

Table 7.1 Calculation of budgeted production to satisfy the sales budget

	Budget (units)
Opening stock of finished goods	500
Closing stock of finished goods	800
Sales	12,400
To satisfy sales would need:	
Opening stock	500
Production	11,900
	12,400

Table 7.2 The production budget

	Units
Made to resell	11,900
Made to stock	800
Production budget	12,700

The cash budget

The diagram about budget interrelationships, Figure 7.3, which we have just looked at, clearly illustrates that the cash budget (also called a 'cash flow forecast') interacts with numerous other budgets. A common cause of business failure has been identified as poor cash flow management. The cash budget is a very important and integral part of good cash flow management. Cash budgeting aims to do the following:

- Make sure that cash is available when it is needed.
- Identify shortages in good time, so that appropriate remedial action can be taken.
- Identify surpluses of cash, so that where possible they can be transferred/invested where they can earn a satisfactory return. Nowadays, the **treasury function** of a company/organization deals with the investment of surplus cash in the short term, e.g. overnight or for, say, a week or a month.

The cash budget is drawn up using predetermined figures. It records them during the month in which they are expected to come in or go out. In doing this it has to take periods of credit allowed by suppliers or to customers into account. So, for example, it does not really matter about the month in which a sale is made or the period covered by a dividend received. What does matter is when the cash from the sale or the dividend is actually received. Thus, non-cash items, e.g. depreciation, are not included in the cash budget. The cash moves when the asset is paid for, not when it is depreciated.

We will now take you through a step-by-step example, which will show you how the cash budget is prepared.

Example 7.2 A cash budget

Brendug and Co. Ltd

1. First of all we have to estimate the cash flows for the forthcoming period, taking into account past performance, future plans and relevant data. Let us assume that this has now been done for Brendug and Co. Ltd and the information generated is as given in Table 7.3.
2. Insert the opening balance for the period. (Our example is a start-up situation, so this does not apply.)

Table 7.3 Brendug and Co. Ltd: cash budget data

20X3

January During this month the company planned to commence trading and receive cash of £100,000 from an issue of £1 ordinary shares.

January To pay £48,000 for plant and machinery. This will be depreciated at 10% of cost per annum.

January To pay a half-year's rent in advance of £12,000.

Sales would be £8,000 in January and then £16,000 per month thereafter. Customers (i.e. debtors) would be given *two months' credit*.

Purchases of raw materials would be £6,000 in January and then £12,000 per month thereafter. Suppliers (i.e. creditors) will only allow *one month's credit*.

Wages and general expenses have been estimated to be £3,000 per month, payable during the month in which they are incurred.

The budgeted closing stock of raw materials is £6,000.

Table 7.4 Brendug and Co. Ltd: cash budget (1) (£000)

	Inflows			Outflows				
	Opening balance	Share capital	Sales	Purchases	Rent	Wages & general expenses	Fixed assets	Closing balance
Jan	–	100	–	–	12	3	48	
Feb	–		–	6	–	3	–	
Mar	–		8	12	–	3	–	
Apr	–		16	12	–	3	–	
May	–		16	12	–	3	–	
Jun	–		16	12	–	3	–	

Table 7.5 Brendug and Co. Ltd: calculating the closing balance for January

	£000
Inflows	100
less Outflows (12 + 3 + 48)	63
= Closing balance	37

3. Fill in the above information vertically, column by column, taking into account the periods of credit. The cash budget will then appear as shown in Table 7.4, for the period of six months to 30 June 20X3.

4. Add up the January inflows and subtract the January outflows to calculate the closing balance, as in Table 7.5.

   The closing balance of £37,000 for January is then carried down as the opening balance for February; to this will be added any February inflows and the February outflows will be deducted, as shown in Table 7.6.

Table 7.6 Brendug and Co. Ltd: calculating the closing balance for February

		£
	Opening balance + inflows	37
less	Outflows	9
		28

Table 7.7 Brendug and Co. Ltd: cash budget (2) (£000)

	Inflows			Outflows				
	Opening balance	Share capital	Sales	Purchases	Rent	Wages & general expenses	Fixed assets	Closing balance
Jan	–	100	–	–	12	3	48	37
Feb	37		–	6	–	3	–	28
Mar	28		8	12	–	3	–	21
Apr	21		16	12	–	3	–	22
May	22		16	12	–	3	–	23
Jun	23		16	12	–	3	–	24
	(Step 5)	100	56	54	12	18	48	

This process will be repeated until the closing balance for June has been computed. When it has, the cash budget will then look like Table 7.7.

5. Having worked out the June closing balance of £24,000, we can then add up each column (other than the opening and closing balance columns) as indicated above. Why?
   Although this is not part of the cash budget, we can then use this information together with the outstanding debtors and creditors to produce information for the budgeted profit and loss account and balance sheet. This will help you understand:

   ☐ The difference between a cash budget and a budgeted profit and loss account, and
   ☐ The difference between profit and cash.

Notice that we did not use the closing stock of raw materials or deal with any depreciation in the cash budget.

The budgeted profit and loss account and the budgeted balance sheet

We adjust the totals for the cash budget (step 5 in Example 7.1) to provide the figures which we need to produce the budgeted profit and loss account and balance sheet, as shown in Table 7.8.

Table 7.8 Brendug and Co. Ltd: converting cash budget information to provide some of the figures for the budgeted profit and loss account and balance sheet (£000)

Share capital	Sales		Purchases	Rent	Wages & general expenses	Fixed assets
100	56		54	12	18	48
Debtors (2 mth × £16)	32	Creditors (1 mth × £12)	12			
	88		66			

Table 7.9 Brendug and Co. Ltd: budgeted profit and loss account

(£000)		
Sales (£56 received in cash + £32 owing from customers)		88
less Cost of Sales		
Opening stock	–	
add Purchases (£54 in cash + £12 owing to suppliers)	66	
	66	
less Closing stock	6	60
Gross profit		28
less Expenses:		
Rent	12	
Wages and general expenses	18	
Depreciation of plant and machinery	2.4	32.4
Net profit (Loss)		(4.4)

Taking into account the closing stock of £6,000 and depreciation of £2,400 (£48,000 × 10% for half a year) we can now draft the budgeted profit and loss account, as shown in Table 7.9.

Finally, we can list all of the budgeted balances as at 30 June 20X3 to produce the budgeted balance sheet (see Table 7.10).

The master budget

You should note that the cash budget, budgeted profit and loss account, and the budgeted balance sheet are frequently referred to as the **master budget**. If management approves it, it will be implemented. If it is not approved, then it is back to the drawing board to review and revise targets, policies, etc. The master budget, once approved, is the culmination of the budget preparation process.

Table 7.10 Brendug and Co. Ltd: budgeted balance sheet

	£000	£000
EMPLOYMENT OF CAPITAL		
Fixed assets:		
Plants and machinery	48	
less Depreciation	2.4	45.6
Working capital		
Current assets:		
Stock	6	
Debtors (2 months × £16)	32	
Cash and bank (per cash budget)	24	
	62	
less **Current liabilities**		
Creditors (1 month × £12)	12	50
		95.6
CAPITAL EMPLOYED		
Share capital	100	
Reserves		
Retained profits (loss)	(4.4)	95.6

Self-assessment Question 7.2

The difference between profit and cash

Now compare the cash budget in Table 7.7 (Example 7.2) with the budgeted profit and loss account of Brendug and Co. Ltd and explain why the cash balance of £24,000 differs from the loss of £4,400. You will find the answer to this assessment on pages 122–3.

SELF-assessment Question 7.3

Having completed the above self-assessment question now see if you can prepare a cash budget, budgeted profit and loss account and balance sheet for Jeanles Ltd.

Jeanles Ltd

Jeanles Ltd are to commence trading in a few months' time on 1 January 20X4 with cash from issued share capital of £60,000. They have provided you with estimates relating to their first six months (Table 7.11).

Prepare a cash budget for the half-year to 30 June 20X4, a budgeted profit and loss account for the half-year and a budgeted balance sheet as at 30 June 20X4.

You will find the suggested answer on pages 123–4.

Table 7.11 Jeanles Ltd: cash budget data

	£	
Quarterly rent of premises, payment due in January and April	1,400	(per quarter)
Cash outlay on equipment – payable January	59,000	
payable March	16,000	
Monthly planned purchase of stock for resale:		
January	10,000	
February	15,000	
March–June (per month)	21,000	

All stock is bought on two months' credit
(i.e. January purchases are paid for in March)

Monthly planned sales are:		
January	8,000	
February	20,000	
March–June (per month)	28,000	

All sales are on one month's credit. No bad debts or arrears of payments are expected. The budgeted closing stock for 30 June 20X4 should be £4,000.

The monthly cash outlay on general expenses is expected to be £500, and wages and salaries are expected to be £1,000 per month. Depreciation of equipment is to be at 20% of cost per annum. The agreed overdraft limit is £7,500.

Flexible budgets

A company/organization can use either a fixed budget or a flexible budget. A fixed budget is a budget which is designed to remain unchanged irrespective of the level of activity (i.e. level of output) actually attained, whereas a flexible budget is a budget which, by recognizing the differences between fixed, semi-fixed and variable costs, is designed to change in relation to the level of activity attained. An example of a flexible budget is shown in Table 7.12.

Table 7.12 Monthly departmental flexible budget

	£000	£000	£000	£000	£000
Sales	80	90	100	110	120
Direct costs (e.g. finished goods, wages)	24	27	30	33	36
Variable overheads	8	9	10	11	12
Semi-fixed overheads	5	6	7	8	9
Fixed overheads	15	15	15	15	17 (step)
	52	57	62	67	74
Profit	28	33	38	43	46

A fixed budget is not really suitable for comparing performance because you could be comparing two completely different levels of activity. The idea behind flexible budgeting is to overcome that problem so that the actual level of activity attained can be compared with a budget appertaining to the same level of activity.

Example 7.3 Fixflex plc

We have been supplied with the information given in Table 7.13. If we compare these figures we will see that a significant proportion of the variances is a direct result of comparing two different levels of activity, i.e. a budget of 30,000 units with an actual performance of 25,000 units.

Taking cost behaviour into account we can recompute (i.e. *flex*) the budget to the actual level achieved and this will provide us with a more realistic and valid comparison, as given in Table 7.14.

The aim of this section is for you to appreciate how flexible budgets are constructed and understand why a business/organization should use them. It is not the intention that you should become proficient in the 'number crunching' aspect of flexible budgeting.

Table 7.13 Fixflex plc: budget/actual information

	Budget August 20X4	Actual August 20X4
Production (units)	30,000	25,000
	£	£
Labour – variable	36,000	33,000
Variable overheads	4,500	3,625
Fixed overheads	5,400	5,400

Table 7.14 Fixflex plc: budget/actual comparative statement

		Budget August 20X4 Per unit £	25,000 units £	Actual August 20X4 25,000 units £	Variance £
Labour	$\dfrac{(£36,000)}{(30,000)}$	1.20	30,000	33,000	(3,000)
Variable overheads	$\dfrac{(£4,500)}{(30,000)}$	0.15	3,750	3,625	125
Fixed overheads		–	5,400	5,400	–
			39,150	42,025	2,875

Note: The fixed costs are assumed to remain unchanged in this example.

The behavioural aspects of budgeting

Budgeting takes place within a human environment and behavioural factors cannot be pushed aside and ignored. Budgets are in fact designed to affect people's behaviour. However, people do not always respond as expected. Their response could be affected by the way in which the budget was drawn up; their involvement/lack of involvement in the preparation of the budget; the way in which it was communicated; their education and training; the way in which the budget is to be implemented; and so on. Some of the causes of the behavioural problems relating to budgeting which are frequently encountered in a company/organization are as follows:

☐ *Perceptions*

Perceptions about the objectives of a company/organization and the interpretation of policy. This is caused by poor communications and a lack of participation.

☐ *Personal goals*

Those who have to abide by the budget, and achieve the targets set, also have their own personal objectives. These personal objectives may conflict and run counter to the objectives laid down by management. For example, departmental heads may become too preoccupied with their own advancement and empire-building, at the expense of achieving budget targets.

☐ *Participation*

A principle of budgeting that is sometimes overlooked, which results in those who should be involved and consulted deciding to withdraw their full-hearted cooperation and support. They may even fail to point out something to management which could well have saved a lot of money and a great amount of time dealing with unnecessary problems.

☐ *Aspiration levels*

The achievement of the budget is perceived or treated as success and non-achievement perceived or treated as failure. This can affect *motivation and morale*.

☐ *Targets*

If targets are set too high, employees may opt out of trying to achieve them. However, if they are set too low, e.g. in an incentive scheme, employees may agree between themselves what the level of production should be! This is because they are afraid that targets will be revised if managers realize they have set the targets too low.

☐ *Obsession*

Some managers are obsessed by the idea that the budget must be achieved at all costs. This is partly due to their aspirations and an uncalled-for perception of accuracy. Some managers tend to forget that the budgeted figures are only estimates.

☐ *An excuse*

If things do go wrong, e.g. where there are organizational problems, it is not uncommon for the budget to get the blame. And if some managers/supervisors wish to justify something which has to be done, they say 'Oh well, we have to do this to keep within our budget'. This then leads their subordinates to treat the budget as a whipping post.

☐ *Resource allocation*
   This is always an area in which conflict can arise, possibly as a result of departmental goals/empire-building.

☐ *Imposition*
   If management imposes budgets 'from above', i.e. a 'top down' approach, the personnel who 'work below' may reject them and fail to pledge their support or generally just show a lack of enthusiasm.

☐ *Sub-optimal decisions*
   If budgets have to be cut, an across-the-board cut will weaken both the strong and the weak! Again, this will undoubtedly result in conflict.

Management therefore needs to tread very carefully when preparing and introducing budgets. To some extent success will depend upon the way in which managers deal with the education and training of other employees, employee participation, good clear communications and the regular review and monitoring of behavioural factors.

The benefits of budgeting

Effective budgeting improves efficiency in that it demands the following:

☐ Careful planning and the provision of information/data for management.
☐ The participation of both management and workers.
☐ Coordination and cooperation.
☐ A sound accounting system.
☐ That new trends and inefficiencies are detected at an early stage of the planning/control process.
☐ The delegation of duties/authority. This will mean that job specifications will have to be clear and unambiguous.
☐ Control by responsibility.
☐ Management by exception.
☐ A sound evaluation system for comparing/reporting on budgeted and actual results.
☐ The motivation of the work force.
☐ Good clear communications.
☐ Corrective action by management to remedy adverse situations.

This can happen only if all those who are involved understand what budgeting is trying to do and are able to express their views during the budget preparation process, and if the budget is flexible enough to take account of changes in circumstances.

Zero base budgeting

Another approach to budgeting is that of zero base budgeting (ZBB). This has been found to be particularly useful in service/support areas, e.g. canteen, welfare, research and development. It forces the managers who are responsible for budgets to justify them and to rank them according to their importance, and also to evaluate more/less costly alternatives. Top management can then screen and discuss the proposals and decide which ones will go ahead. This, it is claimed, promotes a much more efficient allocation of resources. This is because managers have to justify the following:

- ☐ How much they want.
- ☐ Why they want it.
- ☐ How else they could achieve the same result.
- ☐ The degree of importance which they attach to it.

Summary: budgeting and budgetary control

Managerial aspects

Budgeting is a management technique. Management needs to set objectives and formulate policy. The budgets provide targets which reflect the objectives, and the policy is the means by which those targets should be achieved. Management must see that the targets which are set are fair, reasonable and attainable. To produce effective budgets managers must do the following:

- ☐ Secure the cooperation and participation of employees, e.g. supervisors, and certain shop-floor workers.
- ☐ Communicate clearly and indicate acceptance of the budget.
- ☐ Possess negotiation/inter-personal skills and be able to cope with behavioural problems.
- ☐ Delegate the authority and responsibility for budgets to subordinates.
- ☐ Plan the budget preparation process well in advance of the forthcoming budget period, e.g. timetables for meetings, etc. The aim is to ensure that the budget is ready to be implemented before the start of the new budget period.
- ☐ Host/attend the appropriate meetings at which their own budget/certain other budgets will be reviewed/discussed.
- ☐ Appoint a person to act as budget controller.
- ☐ Set up an effective monitoring and reporting system to compare budgeted with actual results at frequent intervals.
- ☐ Be prepared to take action to put right something which is going wrong, as indicated by the feedback from comparative statements/reports.

Budget preparation

It is essential that the budget preparation process commences well before the budget period to which it relates and that the principal budget factor (i.e. a constraint) is identified. The preparation process will be coordinated by the budget controller. The authority and responsibility for a particular budget/section of a budget will be delegated to a named individual. The budget controller will supply that person with appropriate information/ data to help with their budget preparation. From the outset all those involved will have to be issued with instructions and a timetable. The timetable will state when schedules and other information will be required and the dates and times of meetings. Meetings are needed to plan, discuss, review and revise the budgets, to ensure that everything fits together. This is because budgets are interrelated. One budget cannot be prepared in isolation and without reference to the other budgets. When the process is complete, managers must ensure that the information on objectives, policy, targets, etc. is communicated to the appropriate personnel, which indicates managers' acceptance of the budget.

Budgetary control

Control in budgeting is exercised by regular comparisons (e.g. monthly) between budgeted and actual results. The statements/reports produced inform management of where in their company/organization things are not going according to plan. Management can then decide on the form of corrective action which needs to be taken (see Figure 7.4).

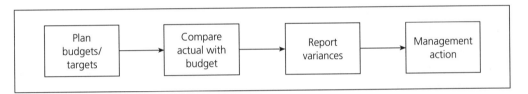

Figure 7.4 Budgetary control

Cost control

Management will be particularly interested in the significant adverse variances which will be highlighted in statements and reports. This system, which singles out those variances which management should look at very carefully, is known as *management by exception*. Managers spend their time and energy putting right things which are going wrong and keeping the company/organization on course to achieve its objectives. Frequent comparisons do provide an early warning system/early detection system of inefficiencies, the emergence of new trends and environmental changes.

Control is also exercised by delegating to an individual the responsibility for a particular budget or subsection of a budget, i.e. *control by responsibility*. That person alone has to justify and explain to management why targets have hot been achieved.

However, if the reported variances are to be any use it is essential that the budgeted and actual figurers have been computed the same way and relate to the same level of activity. This is why, if at all possible, a flexible budget should be used, i.e. a budget which is designed to change as the level of activity changes.

Finally, remember that control should be directed towards problem solving and not the creation of conflict!

More effective budgeting

If budgeting is to become really effective it must be remembered that it is only a forecast. The budget itself, once implemented, must be monitored at frequent intervals, and if necessary amended to take account of changes in the basic assumptions upon which it was based.

Management will also have to monitor *behavioural factors* on a regular basis. People problems, if allowed to fester and multiply, can become the principal reason for the non-attainment of budget targets.

Staff education can be a most worthwhile investment. If staff know more about budgeting and what it is trying to do then, provided that they are able to *participate* and express their opinions, more reasonable, accurate and realistic budgets should be produced.

The master budget

This consists of the following:

☐ A cash budget.
☐ A budgeted profit and loss account.
☐ A budgeted balance sheet.

It is the coming together of all the component parts of the budgeting jigsaw. It communicates in advance of the budget period commencing (e.g. a six- or twelve-month period) the outcome in terms of cash flow, profits, assets and liabilities, etc.

Zero base budgeting

This provides a system of ranking budget packages according to their importance and is suitable for services/non-profit making activities.

Further reading

Drury, J.C., *Management Accounting for Business Decisions*, International Thomson Business Press, 1997.
Horngren, C.T., Foster, G. and Srikant, M.D., *Cost Accounting, A Managerial Emphasis*, Prentice Hall, 2000.
Hussey, J. and Hussey, R., *Cost and Management Accounting*, Macmillan, 1998.

8

An introduction to standard costing

Objectives

When you have worked through this chapter you should be able to:

- [ ] Understand what a standard is, and some of the considerations involved in its composition.
- [ ] Appreciate that a cost variance can be subdivided into a price variance and a quantity variance.
- [ ] Understand why a variance is either adverse or favourable.
- [ ] Appreciate the kind of information which should be given in variance analysis reports and statements.
- [ ] Compute simple labour and material variances.
- [ ] Define some of the variances in your own words.
- [ ] Know some of the causes of labour variances and material variances.

However, please note it is not the intention of this chapter that you become an expert in dealing with the numbers involved. The principal aims are simply that you should be able to follow the workings and understand the principles involved.

What are standard costs?

A standard cost is a predetermined target cost designed to provide a yardstick against which to measure actual performance. The setting of a standard may involve consideration of quantities, prices, rates of pay, qualities and a detailed review of all the relevant factors. Standards can be set for selling prices and the elements of cost, i.e. materials, labour and overheads.

Cost control using standard costing

Control in standard costing is achieved by variance analysis. Figure 8.1 should help you to understand how variance analysis works. At the end of the period under review the actual

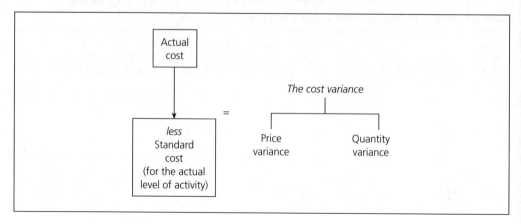

Figure 8.1 Variance analysis

Table 8.1 Variances: materials, labour, overheads and sales

	Total/cost variance	Price variance	Quantity variance
Materials	Material cost variance	Material price variance	Material usage variance
Labour	Labour cost variance	Labour rate variance	Labour efficiency variance
Overheads	Overhead cost variance	Overhead expenditure variance	Overhead volume or efficiency variance
Sales	Sales margin variance	Sales margin price variance	Sales margin volume variance

cost is compared with the predetermined standard cost for the actual level of activity which was attained. This difference is known as the 'total or cost variance'. All variances are the result of two factors, price and quantity. Thus, the total or cost variance can be subdivided into that part of the variance which arises from price differences and that part which arises from differences in quantities. The names of these subvariances may cause confusion, but the principles remain unchanged. Table 8.1 should make the position a little clearer.

Variance analysis – reports and statements

The reports and statements should be presented to management at frequent intervals and indicate which variances are:

☐ *Adverse (or negative)*: e.g. spending more than planned.
☐ *Favourable (or positive)*: e.g. spending less than planned.

If at all possible, they should also distinguish between those variances which are controllable, i.e. those which management can do something about, and those variances which

Table 8.2 Control by responsibility: variance analysis

Variance	Responsible person
Labour efficiency variance	Production manager or departmental manager or supervisor
Material price variance	Chief buyer

are uncontrollable, i.e. where management can do nothing or very little. In practice, management does tend to have more control over quantity variances and less control over price variances.

The reports/statements should also attempt to:

☐ Highlight significant controllable adverse variances.
☐ Inform management of the reasons why certain variances have occurred.

The highlighting of variances is an example of management by exception. Managers can then focus on resolving the problems identified. They can focus their time, attention and expertise on deciding the form of any corrective action which needs to be taken.

The operation of a control by responsibility policy is another important part of the process. Specific members of the work force will need to take on the responsibility for particular variances (for examples see Table 8.2).

Material variances

To illustrate the numbers side of standard costing and to continue what is intended to be a gentle introduction to the subject, we will now take a look at an example. We will work out the figures and then take a step back and look carefully at what they actually mean.

Example 8.1 Material variances

The standard cost of material used for the budget of 10,000 units of product K, for Period 3, 20X2 was:

30,000 kilos (i.e. 3 kilos per unit) @ £2 per kilo = £60,000

Actual production of product K for Period 3, 20X2 was:

8,000 units which took 26,000 kilos of material at a cost of £1.85 per kilo = £48,100

Answer
The first think which you should note is that the budgeted level of activity (i.e. production output) is 10,000 units and the actual level of activity is 8,000 units. To compare our actual costs for 8,000 units with the standard for 10,000 units is incorrect. Why? Because we need to compare the standard and actual costs for the same level of activity: we need to

Table 8.3 Material variances

	Material cost variance £	Material price variance £	Material usage variance £
Actual material used at actual price (26,000 kilos @ £1.85)	48,100	48,100	
Standard material used (for actual level of activity) at standard price (24,000 kilos @ £2)	48,000		48,000
Actual material used at standard price (26,000 kilos @ £2)		52,000	52,000
	100	3,900	(4,000)
	(adverse)	(favourable)	(adverse)

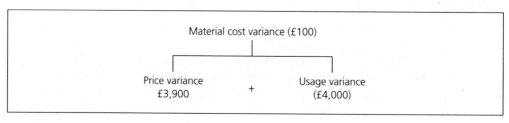

Material cost variance (£100)

Price variance £3,900   +   Usage variance (£4,000)

Figure 8.2 Material variances

compare like with like. Thus we need to calculate the standard cost for the actual level of activity and use that in our calculations, as follows:

8,000 units × 3 kilos per unit = 24,000 kilos @ £2 = £48,000

The second point which you need to note is that the actual price paid of £1.85 for the material is 15p per kilo less than the standard price of £2. Thus, you know from the outset that your price variance is going to be favourable. From this information you can see that the actual material used (26,000 kilos) is greater than the standard, i.e. the planned, use of materials (24,000 kilos) by 2,000 kilos. Using more material than planned in this way is called an adverse material usage variance.

For the calculations see Table 8.3 and for the proof see Figure 8.2.

Self-assessment Question 8.1

By looking at the above calculations, see if you can define in your own words, what is meant by:

1. The material cost variance.
2. The material price variance.
3. The material usage variance.

When you have completed your attempt, compare your answer with the suggested answer on pages 125–6.

What factors will be taken into account when computing the standard material cost? The determination of the standard material cost involves:

☐ *Material quantities (material utilization)*
You will need to consider maximum economies in material usage (assisted by the designers and other appropriate personnel); the setting of standard sizes and standard losses; waste, etc.

☐ *Material prices*
You will need to consider the efficiency of store-keeping and purchasing; forecasts of average prices of materials for future periods, allowing for discounts, carriage and handling charges; information and advice from the purchasing department; and the analysis of trends.

☐ *Quality*
You will need to pay attention to design department recommendations/stipulations; appearance, strength; quality policy; range of materials available; setting of machines and equipment; material specifications; the question of whether to make or buy the components, etc.

The calculation of the subvariances

Managers, executives and students frequently ask for an explanation as to why we calculate the subvariances in the following way:

Price variance
(Actual Price less Standard Price) × Actual Quantity
or
(Actual Price × Actual Quantity) less (Standard Price × Actual Quantity)

Quantity variance
(Actual Quantity less Standard Quantity*) × Standard Price
or
(Actual Quantity × Standard Price) less (Standard Quantity* × Standard Price)

This is best explained by reviewing Figure 8.3 from which you can clearly observe the two subvariances and the way in which they are calculated. Remember also that the two subvariances when added together should equal the total (cost) variance that has been arrived at by comparing:

(Actual Price × Actual Quantity) less (Standard Price × Standard Quantity*)

---

* This should be the standard quantity for the actual level of activity (output).

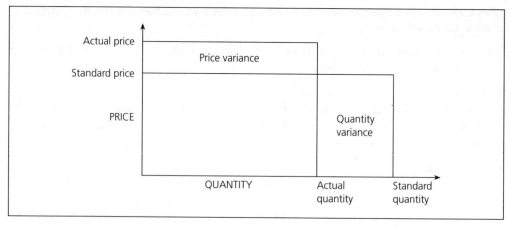

Figure 8.3 The subvariances

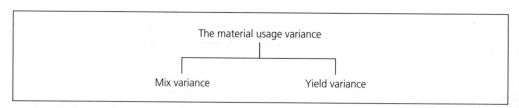

Figure 8.4 Material mix and yield variances

Other material variances

It should be remembered that the material usage variance can, where appropriate, be subdivided further into a mix variance and a yield variance (see Figure 8.4), e.g. in the chemicals industry. This will involve sorting out a standard recipe which stipulates the quantities of each material required and the assessment of a standard yield which takes into account anticipated processing losses.

What can cause a materials price variance? Some of the reasons for a materials price variance are:

☐ Supplier's price change/using a new supplier.
☐ Loss/reduction of trade discount.
☐ Purchase of a different quality from that which was planned.

What can cause a material usage variance?

☐ The quality of the material being used, different from that which was planned.
☐ Pilferage.
☐ Inefficient production workers/methods.
☐ Using unskilled workers to do skilled work.

Labour variances

We will now take a look at labour variances by working through the following self-assessment.

Self-assessment Question 8.2

Using the following information, see if you can complete the variance calculations on the work sheet provided (Figure 8.5).

☐ Standard labour rate: £8.
☐ Hours: 2 hours per component.

The following are actual production data:

☐ 1,000 components produced.
☐ Labour rate: £8.50.
☐ 1,950 hours worked.

WORK SHEET

Standard costing
labour variances

	Labour cost variance £	Labour rate variance £	Labour efficiency variance £
Actual hours @ actual rate	☐	☐	
Standard hours @ standard rate for actual level of activity	☐		☐
Actual hours @ standard rate		☐	☐
	£ ⎯⎯	£ ⎯⎯	£ ⎯⎯

(State whether it is adverse or favourable)

Summary (proof)   £

Labour rate variance
Labour efficiency variance
= labour cost variance   ⎯⎯⎯⎯

Figure 8.5 Standard costing labour variances

Now check your answer with the suggested answer/additional notes on pages 126–7.

What factors will need to be taken into account when calculating the standard cost of labour? The calculation of the standard cost of labour involves a thorough analysis of operations, and possibly a grading review. In order to ascertain the standard labour costs it is necessary to decide upon:

☐ *Labour quantities*
The setting of standard times may be by:
- using past performance records, e.g. the payroll analysis.
- test runs/work study, allowing for fatigue and unavoidable losses.

Standard times could be set for each grade of labour for each cost centre/department.

☐ *Labour rate standard and grades of labour*
Analysis of all factors likely to affect wage rates will help to foretell the actual rate which should be paid during the next period, e.g. a year. The personnel department should be able to provide most of the information. Other factors such as bonus payments, piece rates, overtime premiums, etc. will have to be taken into account.

☐ *Labour grades*
Skills required and operations involved, volume of work, division and availability of labour should all be considered. The work study and personnel departments should combine to provide these data. Other factors such as sex, age, apprenticeship details, etc. should also be reviewed.

Labour rate variances may be caused by the following:

☐ A rate increase, different from that which was anticipated.
☐ Using a different grade of worker, e.g. using a skilled worker to do a semi-skilled operation.
☐ Overtime/bonus and shiftwork payments.

The causes of a labour efficiency variance could be as follows:

☐ Idle (non-productive) time, e.g. training a new operative resulting in lower productivity, machine breakdown, waiting for work or materials, etc.
☐ Poor working conditions, e.g. too hot, too cold, etc.
☐ Behavioural factors, e.g. where employees decide to keep output at a certain level because they are afraid that to produce more may result in the management amending their bonus scheme.
☐ Using a different grade of labour from that which was planned.

The profit variance

There are many more variances than those we have reviewed. To look at all of these other variances in depth is outside the scope of this publication. The variance analysis diagram (Figure 8.6) shows how certain of the variances, e.g. overheads, can be subdivided to provide a more detailed analysis. It also shows that the net difference between all the variances is the profit variance. The profit variance is the actual profit for the period as compared with the standard profit for the actual level of activity attained.

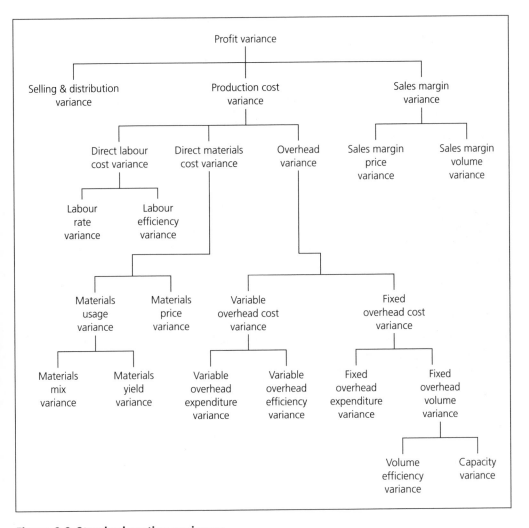

Figure 8.6 Standard costing variances

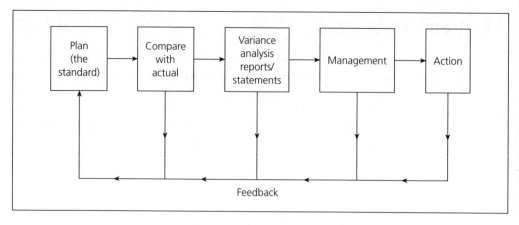

Figure 8.7 Cost control using standard costing

Summary: standard costing

Cost control using standard costing

Cost control is exercised in standard costing via variance analysis. Figure 8.7 should help you to see where it fits into the cost control picture. The predetermination of the standards for materials, labour, overheads and sales involves the consideration of numerous factors/data.

Standard costing developed as a result of the quest for a yardstick against which to measure/compare actual performance. A standard is, therefore, a predetermined target cost or target revenue.

Variance analysis

The comparison of standard with actual results should take place at frequent intervals, e.g. monthly. The variances can be:

☐ Adverse (or negative) e.g. where the actual expenditure exceeds the standard expenditure.
☐ Favourable (or positive) e.g. where the actual expenditure is less than the standard expenditure.

Sales variances will be the other way around. The variances can be further segregated according to whether their causes are controllable or uncontrollable.

The variance analysis in the form of reports and statements supplied to management should:

☐ Highlight controllable adverse variances. This follows the principle of management by exception. Managers are free to concentrate their time and talents towards solving problems which can have a dramatic impact upon performance. This should mean that any necessary corrective action is taken at the earliest available opportunity. It also means that managers are using their valuable time more productively.

☐ Identify and communicate the causes of certain variances.

The reports and statements should be circulated to all those who are responsible for the particular variance. This control by responsibility, i.e. allocating responsibility for each variance to a particular person (e.g. the labour efficiency variance for machine group Z21 to the person in charge of that machine group), ensures that the personnel involved are all striving to keep their costs under control.

Computing the variances

The cost (total) variance is the difference between the standard cost (for the actual level of activity) and the actual cost. This can be subdivided into two subvariances, as shown in Figure 8.8 (see also Table 8.1), price and quantity.

The price variance is the result of paying different actual prices from the prices/rates which were planned, i.e. the standard.

The quantity variance, over which management tends to have more control, is the difference between what the company/organization planned to use, i.e. the standard usage, and the actual quantity which was used. Taken together, the price and quantity variances add back to the cost variance, which provides a quick arithmetic check on the accuracy of the figures. Finally, it must be recognized that standards are only estimates! They must, therefore, be carefully monitored – hence the need for constant feedback (see Figure 8.7) – and revised accordingly.

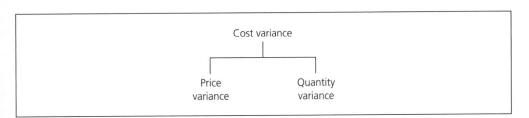

Figure 8.8 Variance analysis: the two subdivisions

Further reading

Drury, C., *Management Accounting for Business Decisions*, International Thomson Business Press, 1997.
Horngren, C.T., Alnoor, B., Foster, G. and Datar, S.M., *Management and Cost Accounting*, Prentice Hall Europe, 1998.
Weetman, P., *Management Accounting*, Financial Times Prentice Hall, 1999.

9

Capital investment appraisal

Objectives

On completion of your study of this chapter, you should be able to:

☐ Understand what relevant/incremental cash flows are.
☐ Understand how the payback and average rate of return methods of capital investment appraisal work.
☐ Know the difference between compound interest tables, the sum of an annuity of £1 tables, the present value of £1 tables and the present value of an annuity of £1 tables.
☐ Use the present value of an annuity of £1 and present value of £1 tables to solve some introductory problems.
☐ Carry out an elementary sensitivity analysis.
☐ Appreciate that there are limitations to all of the methods demonstrated.

The principal aim of this chapter is to show you how to use the present value tables to produce information which will help management with its capital investment decision making. Please note that some authors refer to capital investment appraisal as **capital budgeting** or **project appraisal** or **discounted cash flow**.

Relevant/incremental cash flows

The costs/revenues which need to be used for decision-making purposes should be **relevant costs/revenues** (some authors refer to these as 'incremental costs/revenues').

Which costs and revenues are relevant to a decision? The short answer is 'only those costs and revenues which arise as a direct result of going ahead with the project under review'.

Sunk costs

Sunk costs are those costs which have already been paid out before the specific project under review was ever considered. For example, the cost of a machine purchased some time before the project was first thought of but which is to be used for the project is irrelevant. The machine will be there whether or not the project goes ahead, i.e. the money used to buy it was **sunk** at the time of its purchase. You should, therefore, remember that sunk costs are irrelevant when estimating cash flows/assessing projects.

However, it is not always quite so simple!

Example 9.1

See if you can assess the relevant costs/revenues from the following information and then compare your answer with the answer which follows.

A machine, which is not being used at present, cost £120,000 six years ago. It has a current residual value (i.e. resale value) of £25,000 and would be used for the project under review. At the end of the project it would have a residual value of £7,000.

Answer
The cost of £120,000 for the machine is irrelevant. It is a sunk cost. If the project goes ahead, the current residual value of £25,000 is lost, but at the end of the project £7,000 will be received. The relevant calculation is given in Table 9.1.

Note that if present value tables were to be used, the £25,000 and the £7,000 would have to be dealt with separately. This aspect should become clearer to you when you have studied the remainder of this chapter.

Table 9.1 Calculation of the relevant cost

	£
Residual value lost	25,000
less Residual value at the end of the project	7,000
Relevant cost	18,000

Fixed costs

Fixed costs which have to be paid out whether or not a project goes ahead are irrelevant, e.g. rent of premises, insurance of buildings. However, if additional premises have to be acquired to enable a project to go ahead then the cost of those additional premises is relevant.

Labour costs

Those wages and salaries which continue to be paid whether or not a project goes ahead are irrelevant. Those which have to be paid as a result of taking on the project are relevant.

Example 9.2

Now see if you can identify the relevant labour costs from the following information:

If the project goes ahead, the supervisor, who is currently paid £15,000 per year, will have to take on extra duties for no extra pay. Additionally, one employee currently earning £12,500 per year will have to be made redundant and paid redundancy pay of £5,600.

Answer

The amount paid to the supervisor is irrelevant to the decision. However, if extra money were paid, the extra amount would be relevant. For the redundant employee there would be a one-off relevant cost of £5,600 redundancy pay and a relevant revenue (i.e. a saving) of £12,500 per year over the life of the project.

Materials

Those which have to be purchased specially for the project are relevant.

Example 9.3

See if you can sort out the relevant material costs from the data provided below:

Materials which are to be used for a project consist of the following:

☐ Material L, which cost £6,200, is already in stock. It has no further use and would cost £400 to dispose of.

☐ Material C, which cost £3,600, is already in stock and could be sold on the open market for £3,000.

☐ Material W, which has to be purchased specially for the project at £7,400.

Answer

Material L: the £6,200 is irrelevant. However, if the project went ahead there would be an incremental saving, i.e. a relevant revenue/saving, of £400 because the company would not have to dispose of it.

Material C: the £3,600 cost is irrelevant but there is an incremental loss, i.e. lost revenue of £3,000, because the material which could have been sold for the £3,000 is to be used on the project.

Material W was bought specially for the project and is a relevant/incremental cost.

Depreciation

Depreciation is not a relevant cash flow. The cash moves when the fixed asset concerned is paid for. Depreciation is a non-cash item.

Lost sales

If, as a result of taking on a project, sales of other products are lost, the relevant costs/revenues will be:

sales revenue lost *less* cost of those lost sales = gross profit lost

Although sales revenue is lost, the cost of producing those goods does not have to be paid out (i.e. an incremental receipt). The net effect is a loss of gross profit.

Cash flows are only relevant if they happen as a direct result of the project going ahead, and also where this results in a lost opportunity.

Payback method

This simple approach looks at how long it takes an investment to repay its initial cost (see Table 9.2 for example).

It can be observed that project P has a payback of four years and project Q has a payback of three years. Management tends to favour those projects which pay back more quickly because the longer a project takes to repay, the greater is the uncertainty. The only certainty about the future is that it will be uncertain! However, this method does not take account of the time value of money, i.e. that over a period of time the value of money tends to go down, e.g. £1 now will be worth less in, say, three years' time.

Table 9.2 The payback method

Cost	Project P £20,000		Project Q £20,000	
Year	Cash flow* £000	Cumulative cash flow £000	Cash flow* £000	Cumulative cash flow £000
1	4	4	6	6
2	6	10	8	14
3	7	17	6	**20**
4	3	**20**	3	23
5	5	25	2	25

* The cash flow generated by the project should be the relevant cash flow.

Average rate of return method

Also called the **unadjusted rate of return** method, this is a somewhat oversimplified method which expresses the average annual net cash flow as a percentage of the original investment (see Table 9.3 for example). This return on investment type method assumes

Table 9.3 The average rate of return method

	Machine R	Machine S
Cost of machine	£100,000	£100,000
Total estimated net cash flow for 7 years (i.e. the life of the project)	£171,500	£190,400
Average annual net cash flow	£24,500	£27,200
Average rate of return	24.5%	27.2%

that the net cash flows generated are the same from year to year. The cash flows from both projects could fluctuate significantly from year to year and also vary significantly between each other, i.e. it does not take into account the timing of the cash flows generated. Here also, the time value of money (the fact that £1 tomorrow will be worth less than £1 today) is ignored.

Accounting rate of return

An accounting return on investment approach could also be used; this expresses the financial accounting profit as a percentage of the initial or average amount of capital invested. This method excludes the time value of money, and ignores relevant costs/ revenue.

How to use annuity tables

When confronted with a number of annuity tables for the first time, managers and executives on short courses, and students, soon begin to ask questions:

☐ What are all these for?
☐ How do we use them?
☐ Why use this table and not that one?
☐ Which of these should we use to discount the cash flows?
☐ What do they tell us?
☐ Which of these do we use for capital investment appraisal?

Let us now have a look at the tables and see if we can provide the answers to the above questions.

The compound interest table (compound sum of £1)

Table 9.4 shows how much an investment of £1 will amount to at a certain fixed rate of interest in a certain number of years' time.

Table 9.4 Compound sum of £1 (extract from tables)

Year	10%	12%	14%	16%	18%	20%
1	1.100	1.120	1.140	1.160	1.180	1.200
2	1.210	1.254	1.300	1.346	1.392	1.440
3	1.331	1.405	1.482	1.561	1.643	1.728
4	1.464	1.574	1.689	1.811	1.939	2.074
5	1.611	**1.762**	1.925	2.100	2.288	2.488
6	**1.772**	1.974	2.195	2.436	2.700	2.986

Table 9.5 Compound interest on £1

		Investment £
Example	Invest £1 today	1.00
End of year 1	Interest @ 10% × £1	0.10
Cumulative		1.10
End of year 2	Interest @ 10% × £1.10	0.11
Cumulative		1.21
End of year 3	Interest @ 10% × £1.21	0.12
Cumulative		1.33p and so on

Table 9.4 tells us how much £1 invested now at, say, 12% will amount to in, say, five years' time, i.e. rate column 12%, year 5 = £1.76p to the nearest 1p, as indicated by the 1.762 which was highlighted. Each year the interest is re-invested and also generates interest as illustrated in Table 9.5.

If you invest a sum of money at a fixed rate of interest for a specific period of time, all you have to do is multiply the sum invested with the appropriate figure given by Table 9.4.

Example 9.4 Compound interest

To invest £1,500 today at 10% for six years would accumulate to £2,658 at the end of the sixth year. This is computed as follows:

Rate 10% for 6 years   Amount invested now
   1.772   ×   £1,500   = £2,658

In addition to working out the amount accumulated, this table can be used to produce an **opportunity cost**, i.e. the value of the benefit forgone. For example, an amount invested in a business project could have alternatively been invested in a bank.

Investing an annual sum (sum of an annuity of £1 for N years)

From a review of Table 9.6 it can be observed that it shows what happens if £1 is invested at the end of each year, at a fixed rate of interest, and for a certain number of years.

Table 9.6 The sum of an annuity of £1 for N years (extract from tables)

Year	10%	12%	14%	16%	18%	20%
1	1.000	1.000	1.000	1.000	1.000	1.000
2	2.100	2.120	2.140	2.160	2.180	2.200
3	3.310	3.374	3.440	3.506	3.572	3.640
4	4.641	4.779	4.921	5.066	5.215	5.368
5	6.105	6.353	6.610	**6.877**	7.154	7.442
6	7.716	8.115	**8.536**	8.977	9.442	9.930

Example 9.5 Investment

An investment of £1, at the end of *each* year for six years (i.e. an annual investment of £1) at 14% would produce £8.54p to the nearest 1p (see Table 9.6). This builds up as shown in Table 9.7.

Notice that the table is drawn up on the assumption that *the investment is made at the end of each year.*

Table 9.7 Compound interest for an annual investment of £1

		Investment
End of year 1	Annual investment	1.00
End of year 2	Interest @ 14% × £1	0.14
	Annual investment	1.00
		2.14
End of year 3	Interest @ 14% × £2.14	0.30
	Annual investment	1.00
		3.44 and so on

If a fixed amount of money is to be invested at the end of each year, the annual amount is multiplied by the appropriate figure given in Table 9.6, according to the rate at which the amount is invested and the length of time involved.

Example 9.6 Investment of £2,000

To invest an annual amount of £2,000 at the end of each year for five years at 16% would compound (i.e. accumulate) to £13,754. This is computed as follows:

Rate 16% for 5 years   Annual investment
        6.877   ×   £2,000   = £13,754

Thus, although the amount invested is only £10,000 (i.e. £2,000 per year × 5 years), it generates an additional £3,754 because of the accumulation of the compound interest.

The present value table (present value of £1)

From a capital investment appraisal point of view, this is the most important and most frequently used table (see Table 9.8).

This table is all about the **time value of money**, i.e. the fact that over a period of time the value of money will tend to decrease.

The table can be looked at in two ways:

1. It shows us *how much we need to invest at a specific fixed rate of interest and for a particular period of time to produce £1*, e.g. if we want to produce £1 at the end of year 1 at a 10% rate of interest we have to invest 90.9p at the beginning of year 1, as follows:

Table 9.8 Present value of £1 (extract from tables)

Year	10%	12%	14%	16%	18%	20%
1	**0.909**	0.893	0.877	0.862	0.847	0.833
2	0.826	0.797	0.769	0.743	0.718	0.694
3	**0.751**	0.712	0.675	0.641	0.609	0.579
4	0.683	0.636	0.592	0.552	0.516	0.482
5	0.621	0.567	0.519	0.476	**0.437**	0.402
6	0.564	**0.507**	0.456	0.410	0.370	0.335

Investment (to nearest 1p) at the start of the year	= 91p
At the end of year (to nearest 1p) interest @ 10% × 91p	= 9p
∴ investment + interest	= £1

Or, if we want to produce £1 in six years at a 12% rate of interest we would have to invest 50.7p now (51p to the nearest 1p). This, together with the compound interest would produce £1 at the end of year 6 (as indicated by the 0.507 figure which is highlighted in Table 9.8).

2. The other way of looking at the table is that it tells us *what the value of £1 receivable in a certain number of years' time, taking into account a specific rate of interest, will be*, i.e. the present value of receiving £1 in the future.

In capital investment appraisal, this philosophy is the one which is followed, as it tends to explain the time value of money. For example, the present value of £1 receivable in five years' time, and taking into account a rate of interest of 18%, is 43.7p (or 44p to the nearest 1p); or the present value £1 receivable in three years' time at a rate of interest of 10% is 75.1p (or 75p to the nearest 1p). (See Table 9.8.)

The value of £1 received today is £1 but if you receive it in the future its value will tend to be less than a pound. The rate of interest could be in line with the rate of inflation or the company/organization's cost of capital or the required rate of return for the type of project which is being reviewed.

The present value of an annuity table

This table can also be used in capital investment appraisal for certain situations (see Table 9.9).

It can also be viewed in two ways:

1. It tells us how much we need to invest now, at a specific fixed rate of interest, to generate £1 at the end of *each* year for a specified number of years. For example, if we wish to receive £1 at the end of each of the next four years, and taking interest into account at 16%, we would have to invest £2.798 (£2.80), i.e. £2.80 invested now at 16% will generate £1 per year at the end of each of the next four years.

Table 9.9 Present value of an annuity of £1 (extract)

Year	10%	12%	14%	16%	18%	20%
1	0.909	0.893	0.877	0.862	0.847	0.833
2	1.736	1.690	1.647	1.605	1.566	1.528
3	2.487	2.402	2.322	2.246	2.174	2.106
4	3.170	3.037	2.914	**2.798**	2.690	2.589
5	3.791	3.605	3.433	3.274	3.127	2.991
6	4.355	4.111	3.889	3.685	3.498	3.326

2. It represents *the present value of receiving the same amount each year for a certain number of years*, and taking interest into account at a specific rate. It can be used to find out the time value of cash flows, but only in cases where the same amount is received each year for a number of years, and is therefore of limited application.

The present value method

In capital investment appraisal, the time value of money is taken into account by revaluing the cash flows at their present values. The appraisal process will involve the following:

☐ The estimation of the cash flows over the life of the project. The cash flows to be estimated should be the **relevant/incremental cash flows**, i.e. they take account only of those items of income or expenditure which come in or go out if the project goes ahead; e.g. if a new employee has to be taken on if a particular project goes ahead, the remuneration paid to the new employee is a relevant/incremental cost.
☐ Taking into account taxation.
☐ Selecting the rate of interest which is to be used as the discount rate. A company/organization could opt for:
  ● the cost of capital; or
  ● a rate which takes into account the risk category of the project (see Table 9.10 for example); or
  ● a cut-off rate. If the net present value of a project's cash flows, as discounted using the cut-off rate, is negative, the project will not go ahead.

We will now proceed to work through a series of problems and self-check assignments to illustrate how the present value tables are used.

Table 9.10 Capital investment appraisal: risk categories

Risk category	Required rate of return
Low	12%
Medium	16%
High	20%

More detailed present value tables can be found in Appendix 2. However, for the examples which follow we will use the table extracts which have been included so far.

Example 9.7 Using the tables

Machinery can be purchased on payment of the following amounts:

☐ £5,000 immediately, and
☐ £2,000 at the end of each of the next four years, and
☐ £4,000 at the end of the fifth year.

Using the appropriate tables, calculate the present value/equivalent cash price which could be offered if payment were to be made in full now. Compound interest needs to be taken into account at 10% per annum.

Answer
It will cost £6,340 at 10% per annum compound interest now to produce the four annual instalments of £2,000 each. £2,484 will need to be invested now at 10% per annum compound interest to generate the £4,000 which will be required at the end of year 5. The calculation is shown in Table 9.11.

Table 9.11 Calculating the equivalent cash price using present value tables

	£
Amount payable immediately	5,000
Present value of an annuity of £2,000 for 4 years @ 10%	
= £2,000 × 3.170 (Table 9.9)	6,340
Present value of £4,000 at the end of 5 years @ 10%	
= £4,000 × 0.621 (Table 9.8)	2,484
Present value (equivalent cash price)	13,824
This is the cost of producing	5,000 now
plus £2,000 × 4 =	8,000
and £4,000 × 1 =	4,000
	17,000

Self-assessment Question 9.1

Now see if you can solve a similar problem which is described in the following.

The equivalent cash price

Your company is considering buying some equipment and has received an offer from one of the suppliers involving the payment of:

☐ £3,000 on delivery, and
☐ £3,000 at the end of each of the next three years, and

☐ £5,000 at the end of year 4, and
☐ £2,500 at the end of year 5.

The interest rate applicable is 12%.
   When you have finished your calculations please turn to page 127 and compare your answer with the suggested answer.

Example 9.8 Cash flows of the same amount per year and depreciation

The forecast incremental receipts and payments applicable to the purchase of a new machine are as shown in Table 9.12.
   The new machine will cost £20,000.

Calculation
First of all we adjust the net income figures for each year, by adding back the depreciation (see Table 9.13).
   Because the cash flows are the same each year, we can use Table 9.9, the present value of an annuity of £1, to discount the cash flows, as follows:

annual net cash flows × discount rate = present value
   £7,000   ×   3.17   = £22,190

We can deduct the initial cost of the project:

less initial investment (£20,000) = **Net present value (NPV) = £2,190**

The NPV is positive and the project is therefore worthy of acceptance/further consideration.

Table 9.12 Identical cash flows

Year	1 £000	2 £000	3 £000	4 £000
Receipts	16	16	16	16
less Payments*	14	14	14	14
Net income	2	2	2	2

* The payments include depreciation at £5,000 per year. The company's cost of capital is 10%.

Table 9.13 Adjusting for depreciation

Year	1 £000	2 £000	3 £000	4 £000
Net income	2	2	2	2
add back Depreciation	5	5	5	5
Net cash flow	7	7	7	7

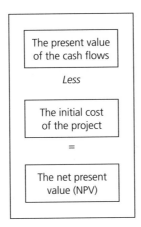

Figure 9.1 The net present value of a project

From the above, it can be observed that the net present value (NPV) of a project is as shown in Figure 9.1.

Self-assessment Question 9.2

Identical cash flows/the treatment of depreciation

If the GT Company go ahead with a new project, it anticipates that its net cash flows (before deducting depreciation) over a six-year period will be £12,000 per annum. The project would involve buying specialized equipment costing £60,000 which would be depreciated at £10,000 per annum and have no residual value at the end of year 6. The cost of capital is 16%.

See if you can calculate the net present value of this project and indicate if it is worthy of further consideration.

When you have completed your attempt at this problem, turn to page 127 and compare it with the suggested solution.

In the real world of business it is more likely that the estimated cash flows which result from taking on a new project will vary from year to year. This means that each individual amount will have to be discounted using the appropriate present value of £1, as illustrated in Table 9.8.

Example 9.9 Fluctuating cash flows

Wys plc is considering purchasing a new robotic machine. The anticipated receipts and payments resulting from its purchase are as shown in Table 9.14.

An immediate cash outlay of £20,000 is needed to finance the purchase. The company's cost of capital is 16%.

Table 9.14 Fluctuating cash flows

Year	1 £000	2 £000	3 £000	4 £000	5 £000
Incremental receipts	14	16	22	12	9
Incremental payments*	11	15	16	10	8

* Includes depreciation of £4,000 per annum.

Table 9.15 The net present value of fluctuating cash flows

Year	Receipts £000	Payments* £0000	Cash flow £000	Discount factor £000	Net present value £000
1	14	7	7	0.862	6.034
2	16	11	5	0.743	3.715
3	22	12	10	0.641	6.410
4	12	6	6	0.552	3.312
5	9	4	5	0.476	2.380
					21.851
		less initial outlay			20.000
		Net present value			**1.851**

* Adjusted for depreciation.

Calculation

See Table 9.15. The NPV is positive, which means that the project is worthy of consideration. Note, that the cash flows had to be adjusted because depreciation had been included in the payment figures.

Discounting the cash flows in this way may also be described as discounted cash flow (DCF).

Why in the above answer did we say 'worthy of consideration' rather than 'acceptable'? The reason for this caution is that the financial data are just one part of the capital-investment, decision-making jigsaw. There are many non-financial factors which have to be taken into account, e.g. reliability, the efficiency of the supplier's after-sales service, standardization, etc.

Now see if you can complete the final activity problem.

Self-assessment Question 9.3

Becwik Ltd

The directors of Becwik Ltd are considering the acquisition of a new machine which could generate incremental cash inflows and outflows as shown in Table 9.16. The immediate initial outlay to acquire the machine and set it up for operations is estimated at £79,000 and it will have no residual value at the end of year 6. (For financial

Table 9.16 Becwik Ltd: incremental cash flows

Year	1 £000	2 £000	3 £000	4 £000	5 £000
Income	40	60	80	80	30
Expenditure before depreciation	30	40	40	30	20
Incremental cash flow	10	20	40	50	10

Table 9.17 Becwik Ltd: risk categories

Risk	Required rate of return
A Low	10%
B Average	14%
C High	18%

accounting purposes new machinery is depreciated on a straight-line basis.) Becwik's corporate planning team has categorized all projects as shown in Table 9.17. The risk category of this project is considered to be average.

You are required to evaluate the project.

When you have attempted to answer the above problem, please turn to page 128 and compare it with the suggested answer.

Residual values

If the machinery or equipment under review has a residual value at the end of the project, this should be included as an additional cash flow for the period in which it is to be received. However, beware! Many examples in numerous texts assume that the residual value will be received at the end of the year in which the project comes to an end. In reality, when the project does come to an end, it may be some time before the machinery or equipment is disposed of. The cash from such a disposal should therefore be included as a cash flow of the year in which it is anticipated that it will be received.

Taxation

In producing the cash flows the tax factor should be taken into account *assuming that the company will be paying tax* as follows:

☐ The tax benefit (i.e. the tax allowance at the tax-paying businesses' rate of tax) should be deducted from the cash flows of the period in which the benefit is received as a repayment or used to reduce the amount of tax which has to be paid over.

☐ The tax payable on income, e.g. taxable cash flows received and taxable profits on the disposal of machinery and equipment, should be deducted from the cash flows received (if any) of the period in which the tax will be actually paid over.

In both of the above cases there is usually a time lag between the period to which the benefit/tax payable relates, and the period which derives the benefit or in which the tax is paid.

Other methods

☐ *Discounted payback*
The payback method referred to earlier in this chapter can also be computed using the present value of the cash flows. The discounted payback period is the time that it takes for the cumulative present value of the cash flows to equal the initial investment.

☐ *Internal rate of return (IRR)*
This is also called the **yield method**: the internal rate of return is the discount rate which will discount the cash flows to a net present value of nil (i.e. the present value of the cash flows less the initial investment = a nil NPV). It is, therefore, a return on investment approach, the IRR being an indication of what a particular project is likely to earn.

Sensitivity analysis

This is a method of assessing the extent to which a change in one or more of the assumptions on which a capital investment project (or a budget) was based would affect the outcome. For example, higher- or lower-than-expected wage settlements, machine running costs, and residual values of plant disposed of could significantly affect the possible outcome.

This enables managers to review a number of possible outcomes, particularly in situations where the exact outcome is difficult to predict, and thereby assists them with their decision making.

Which method?

The methods which use the net present value tables are to be preferred because they all take into account the time value of money. However, it must be stressed that the selection of a discount rate is not always an easy task, e.g. there are a number of ways of calculating a company's cost of capital. With all methods, it must be remembered that the cash flows/ residual values of machinery and equipment are only estimates.

Summary: capital investment appraisal

Relevant/incremental cash flows

The methods described in this chapter all depend upon the predetermination of the cash flows. Thus, you should always be aware that the cash flows used in capital investment appraisal (also called profit appraisal and capital budgeting) are only estimates. Their accuracy will depend upon the data and the validity of the assumptions used in their preparation. The cash flows which are to be used should be relevant/incremental cash flows.

Relevant/incremental cash flows are those that occur as a result of taking on a new project, for example:

- [ ] A new worker has to be employed and paid £15,000 per year.
- [ ] A special maintenance contract has to be purchased at a cost of £24,000 per year.
- [ ] Certain materials have to be purchased.
- [ ] Residual value/scrap value is received at the end of the project's life.
- [ ] Additional fixed costs have to be paid out.

Examples of irrelevant costs are:

- [ ] A feasibility study would have to be paid even if the project does not go ahead.
- [ ] If a supervisor is paid a salary of £28,000 per annum whether or not the project is undertaken.
- [ ] Factory rent and rates which have to be paid whether or not the project under review goes ahead.

Note that, when estimating the cash flows, *depreciation* should be ignored. The cash moves when the fixed asset concerned is paid for. Depreciation is a non-cash item.

The time value of money

This means that £1 tomorrow will be worth less than £1 today. Thus, cash flows which are to be received in the future are not worth as much as they are now.

The financial information provided – a warning

From the outset it should be noted that the financial information provided to management forms just one of the many component parts needed to effectively vet a capital investment proposal. Indeed, there are numerous non-financial factors which have to be taken into account, e.g. efficiency of servicing, reliability, risks associated with buying from overseas suppliers, etc.

The tables

If you are to master capital investment appraisal, you need to be able to use the following:

☐ The present value of £1 table, an extract of which is shown as Table 9.8 in this chapter.
☐ The present value of an annuity of £1 table, an extract of which appears as Table 9.9 in this chapter.

Methods of capital investment appraisal

We can classify the methods of capital investment appraisal/capital budgeting in a number of ways. For this introductory study, I suggest that we simply divide the methods into those which *do not* take into account the time value of money, and those which *do* take into account the time value of money.

Methods which do not take the time value of money into account

☐ *Payback*
This method calculates how long it takes the cash flows generated by a specific project to recover the initial cost of the investment. Those who use this method of evaluation prefer those projects which repay the cost of the initial investment in the shortest time. In estimating the cash flows the earlier cash flows are likely to be more accurate than later cash flows.

☐ *The average rate of return (unadjusted rate of return)*
This return on investment method expresses the average cash flow per year as a percentage of the initial investment. Although it is simple to calculate it must be pointed out that it does ignore the timing of the cash flows, i.e. it averages the cash flows over the life of the project when in fact they could fluctuate quite significantly from year to year.

☐ *Accounting rate of return*
This method uses financial accounting profits.

Each of the above methods suffer because they ignore the time value of money. Also, the timing of the cash flows, i.e. the year in which the money comes in or goes out, can have a dramatic impact upon a project.

Methods which take account of the time value of money

☐ *The net present value method*
To find the net present value (NPV) each of the cash flows is multiplied by the appropriate discount factor, using Table 9.8 (the present value of £1 table). These are then added up and the initial investment deducted. If the resulting figure, the NPV, is positive, the project is worthy of consideration; if the NPV is negative, the project should be rejected because it is not a wealth-creating opportunity. Note that when using this method, if all the cash flows are identical, Table 9.9, the present value of an

annuity of £1 table, could be used and would save calculation time. This discounting process may also be called DCF (discounted cash flow).

☐ *The internal rate of return (IRR) or yield method*
Although to produce numerical examples of this is outside the scope of this introduction, it is worth noting that this method is important. Look at any financial management text and you will find out why. The internal rate of return is the discount rate which will produce an NPV of nil, i.e. the cash flows discounted less the initial cost of the machine/equipment/project = nil. Therefore projects with an IRR greater than the company's normal discount rate appropriate to the particular project under review are well worth further investigation.

☐ *Discounted payback*
This method simply calculates the payback using the discounted cash flows.

The above methods which take into account the time value of money are preferable to those which do not.

Taxation

Taxation allowances must be included in the cash flows for the period which benefits from those allowances. Tax payments must be included in the cash flows for the period in which they are to be paid over. Thus care needs to be exercised in taking the tax factor into account by taking the various time lags into account, e.g. the tax on the income of year 1 could be paid in year 2.

Sensitivity analysis

Sensitivity analysis can provide management with a range of possible outcomes resulting from one or more changes in the basic assumptions on which the data used is based.

Further reading

Atrill, P. and McLaney, E., *Financial Management Accounting for Non-specialists*, Financial Times Prentice Hall, 2000.
Chadwick, L. and Kirkby, D., *Financial Management*, International Thomson Business Press, 1995.
Knott, G., *Financial Management*, Macmillan, 1998.
Pike, R. and Neale, B., *Corporate Finance and Investment*, Prentice Hall Europe, 1999.

10

Assessing the financial performance

It is very difficult to define and identify where financial accounting, financial management, cost accounting and management accounting start and finish. They are all interrelated and what one authority calls, for example, a cost accounting topic, other authorities may describe it as either a financial accounting or a management accounting topic! Financial analysis tends to be used by both financial accountants and management accountants.

Objectives

The financial statements which we looked at when we reviewed budgeting and budgetary control, namely, the profit and loss account and the balance sheet, can be subjected to closer interrogation via ratio analysis. The principal aim of this chapter is to introduce you to some of the ratios which will enable you to make an overview of a company's financial performance. When you have completed the chapter you should be able to:

☐ Calculate the ratios which have been included.
☐ Understand the purpose for which the ratios are being calculated.
☐ Use the ratios to prepare a financial analysis based on some accounts and to comment briefly on your findings.
☐ Appreciate the limitations of ratio analysis.

There has and always will be a quest for a 'yardstick', i.e. an objective measure against which to measure performance. Ratio analysis enables objective comparisons to be made with earlier years' figures for the same company and/or other companies, e.g. competitors and/or industry figures relating to the specific sector in which the company operates.

Who to compare with? This is not an easy task. All you can do is try to find another company which:

☐ Has the same year-end, and a similar product portfolio or offers the same or similar types of service(s).
☐ Is of a similar size in terms of turnover and the number of employees.
☐ Finances its assets in a similar way, e.g. some companies have a lot of 'off-balance-sheet financing', i.e. certain fixed assets such as machinery and equipment do not appear on their balance sheets because they have been rented, hired or leased.

☐ Has revalued its fixed assets following a similar timescale.

☐ Uses similar accounting policies, e.g. the policies concerned with the depreciation of fixed assets.

☐ Is located in an area which has a similar cost of living in terms of overheads, such as rents of property, etc.

You can appreciate from your review of the above that a perfect match will be almost an impossibility. All you can do is to select a company or companies which provide a reasonable match. However, you need to be aware of the fact that companies do change their accounting policies from time to time and also change the way in which they finance and/or revalue their assets. The best and most realistic comparison is the ratio analysis which is prepared for internal purposes. However, all comparisons really need to take account of several years' figures (e.g. 5 years') in order to make intelligent judgements and to help identify trends.

Ratio analysis

Ratio analysis is a tool which is used in order to compare and evaluate financial performance. The source data from which the ratios are calculated may be internal, e.g. the company's own profit and loss account, appropriation account, balance sheet and data relating to debtors, creditors and stocks, etc.; or external in the form of the published accounts of other companies and industry figures which are available from a variety of sources.

Ratios can help to do the following:

☐ Indicate areas in which further investigation is needed.
☐ Highlight strengths and weaknesses.
☐ Provoke questions.

Ratios are of little value if they are used in isolation. To be useful, they need to be viewed in conjunction with other data, such as the following:

☐ Information about the management.
☐ Industry figures, which provide a yardstick with which realistic comparisons can be made.
☐ The value of fixed assets and investments.
☐ Opportunity costs, e.g. the returns available from alternative investments.
☐ Government regulations/legislation already passed or pending.
☐ Security, i.e. the degree to which the company has used its assets as security for loans and debentures.

The ratios

The following ratios should help you to make a reasonable assessment of the financial performance of a company.

Profitability

The gross profit to sales ratio is expressed as follows:

$$\frac{\text{Gross profit}}{\text{Sales}} \times 100$$

It indicates the average gross margin (mark-up) which is being made on the products/services which are being sold.

The net profit to sales (net margin) ratio is expressed as follows:

$$\frac{\text{Net profit before tax}}{\text{Sales}} \times 100$$

This shows how much profit is being generated by the sales and in addition to the effects of the gross profit it provides an indication as to what is happening to the overheads.

The return on investment (ROI) ratio also called 'return on capital employed' (ROCE) and 'return on assets' is expressed as follows:

$$\frac{\text{Net profit before interest and tax (NPBIT)}}{\text{Capital employed (less intangibles, if any)}} \times 100$$

This gives the overall return on all of the capital which has been invested in the business, i.e. it is a measure of the productivity of all the capital invested in the business irrespective of its source.

Liquidity ratios

The current ratio (or the ratio of current assets to current liabilities) is expressed as follows:

$$\frac{\text{Current assets}}{\text{Current liabilities}}$$

This provides an indication of whether the company has excess liquidity, satisfactory liquidity or liquidity problems. It provides an indication of the company's ability to pay its short-term debts.

The acid test (or quick) ratio is expressed as follows:

$$\frac{\text{Liquid assets (i.e. current assets less stocks)}}{\text{Current liabilities}}$$

This is a key ratio used in the management of working capital, which looks at the ability to pay short-term debts with the liquid assets. As a general rule, this ratio is expected to be around one-to-one, i.e. £1 of liquid assets to every £1 owing to current liabilities. However, in practice the liquid assets tend to be less than £1 for every £1 owing to current liabilities.

Efficiency ratios

These ratios look at asset utilization and provide an insight into the efficiency of inventory (stock) control and credit control.

The average collection period ratio is expressed as follows:

$$\frac{\text{Average debtors}}{\text{Sales}} \times 365$$

This provides us with an indication of how long it is taking us to collect the amounts owing from our credit customers, i.e. our debtors.

The credit period taken ratio is expressed as follows:

$$\frac{\text{Average creditors}}{\text{Purchases (or sales if the purchases figure is not available)}} \times 365$$

This tells us the average time it takes us to pay our suppliers of goods on credit. Note that creditors do represent a source of short-term financing to the company.

The stock turnover ratio is expressed as follows:

$$\frac{\text{Cost of sales (or sales)}}{\text{Average stock (i.e. opening plus closing stock divided by two)}} = \text{The rate of turnover}$$

This shows the number of times which the average stock held is sold in a given period of time.

The sales to fixed assets ratio is expressed as follows:

$$\frac{\text{Sales}}{\text{Fixed assets}} = \text{The overall efficiency with which the fixed assets are used}$$

or can be expressed using just the manufacturing assets:

$$\frac{\text{Sales}}{\text{Manufacturing fixed assets}} = \begin{array}{l}\text{A measure of the utilization of} \\ \text{manufacturing fixed assets}\end{array}$$

Capital structure ratios

The gearing (or leverage) ratio is expressed as follows:

$$\frac{\begin{array}{c}\text{Debt, i.e. other forms of long-term financing} \\ \text{(with or without the bank overdraft, as appropriate)}\end{array}}{\begin{array}{c}\text{Debt (with or without the bank overdraft) + ordinary share} \\ \text{capital + reserves}\end{array}} \times 100$$

This looks at the proportion of debt and other forms of long-term financing in relation to the total long-term financing and is of particular significance to financial management and the providers of finance.

The debt/equity ratio is expressed as follows:

$$\frac{\text{Debt}}{\text{Equity}}$$

Those companies with a high proportion of debt to equity, i.e. those which are highly geared, tend to be at greater risk in periods where trading conditions are poor. This is because they have to pay interest or repay capital and interest on debentures/loans irrespective of whether they are performing well or badly.

Many companies nowadays do use their bank overdraft as a long-term source of funds. Note that there are many more gearing ratios and that some authors exclude the preference shares from the other forms of long-term financing and treat it in the same way as the equity.

The interest cover ratio is expressed as follows:

$$\frac{\text{Net profit before interest and tax}}{\text{Loan and debenture interest}}$$

This ratio shows how well the company can cover the interest that it has to pay out. It is expressed as the number of times that it can cover the interest payments. If the preference dividend is added to the loan and debenture interest, the ratio then becomes the **fixed charge cover**.

Employee ratios

Employee ratios assess the productivity of labour in terms of sales and net profit, for example:

☐ Average remuneration per employee.
☐ Net profit per employee.
☐ Sales per employee.
☐ Directors' efficiency.

Investment ratios

Investment ratios are of particular significance to directors, shareholders, analysts, would-be investors and competitors.

The earnings/shareholders' equity (return on equity) ratio is expressed as follows:

$$\frac{\text{Net profit after tax, less preference dividends (if any)}}{\text{Equity (i.e. issued ordinary share capital + reserves)}} \times 100$$

This ratio provides the ordinary shareholders with an idea of what their return on investment is. The profit figure which is used in the calculation represents what is left for them after paying everything else including interest and tax, and dividends on preference shares.

The dividend yield ratio can be expressed as follows:

$$\frac{\text{Dividend per ordinary share}}{\text{Market price per ordinary share}} \times 100$$

This ratio relates the profit distributed as dividend to the share price. It does not measure the return on investment for a shareholder because there are also the capital gains on their shares to consider. However, it does provide a potential investor with an indication of the expected rate of return on investment in terms of cash paid out.

The earnings per ordinary share or earnings per share (EPS) ratio is expressed as follows:

$$\frac{\text{Net profit after tax less preference dividend}}{\text{Number of ordinary shares issued}}$$

This represents the earning power per share.

The dividend cover (on ordinary shares) ratio is expressed as follows:

$$\frac{\text{Earnings per share}}{\text{Dividend per share}}$$

This ratio shows how many times the company can cover its ordinary share dividends from its current earnings. It can also be calculated in the following way:

$$\frac{\text{Net profit after tax less preference dividend}}{\text{Total ordinary share dividend}}$$

The price earnings (PE) ratio is expressed as follows:

$$\frac{\text{Market price per ordinary share}}{\text{Earnings per ordinary share}}$$

This ratio expresses the relationship between the company's ability to generate profits and the market price of its ordinary shares.

The capitalization rate (or earnings yield) ratio is the PE ratio turned upside down, and is expressed as follows:

$$\frac{\text{Earnings per ordinary share}}{\text{Market price per ordinary share}} \times 100$$

It provides shareholders and investors with an indication of the current performance of the ordinary shares, i.e. it provides a measure of the cost of the equity share capital.

Example 10.1 Thirstin Leas Ltd

This chapter has provided you with the ratios, i.e. the tools, with which you can analyse and assess company performance. There now follows an example for you to use to check your understanding of the ratios.

Profit and loss account for the year ended 31 December 20X2

		£000	£000
Sales			500
Less	Cost of sales:		
	Stock at 1 January 20X2	40	
	Purchases	300	
		340	
Less	Stock at 31 December 20X2	50	290
			210
	Manufacturing wages		75
	Gross profit		135
Less	Expenses:		
	Selling expenses	25	
	Distribution expenses	10	
	Admin. and financial expenses	40	75
	Net profit before tax		60

Balance sheet as at 31 December 20X2

	£000	£000
Share capital		500
Reserves		250
		750
10% debentures		150
Capital employed		900
Current liabilities:		
Overdraft	15	
Trade creditors (20X1 £35,000)	65	80
		980
Fixed assets		820
Current assets:		
Stock	50	
Debtors (20X1 £60,000)	110	
Bank	–	160
		980

We will now calculate the following ratios:

1. The ordinary shareholders' interest.
2. The working capital.
3. The amount of debenture interest which would have been included in the admin. and financial expenses.

4. The gross profit/sales%.
5. The net profit/sales%.
6. The acid test.
7. Return on capital employed (return on assets).
8. Average collection period.
9. Average credit period taken.
10. The rate of stock turnover.
11. Sales to fixed assets.
12. The gearing (treating the bank overdraft as a current liability).
13. The interest cover.

As we compute each ratio see if you can follow the calculations and ensure that you know where the figures have come from.

Solution: Thirstin Leas Ltd
1. Ordinary shareholders' interest = ordinary share capital plus reserves (i.e. £500 + £250 = £750 (£000s).
2. The working capital = current assets less current liabilities (i.e. £160 − £80) = £80 (£000s).
3. Debenture interest = 10% × £150 = £15 (£000s). Provided that the whole amount had been issued before the start of the year, hence a full year's debenture interest.

4. Gross profit/sales%:

$$\frac{\text{Gross profit}}{\text{Sales}} \times 100 = \frac{135}{500} \times 100 = 27\%$$

Because this was a manufacturing company, the manufacturing wages were treated as part of the cost of sales.

5. Net profit/sales%:

$$\frac{\text{Net profit before tax}}{\text{Sales}} \times 100 = \frac{60}{500} \times 100 = 12\%$$

6. The acid test:

$$\frac{\text{Liquid assets}}{\text{Current liabilities}} = \frac{(160 - 50)}{80} = \frac{110}{80} = 1.375$$

7. Return on capital employed:

$$\frac{\text{Net profit before tax} + \text{debenture interest}}{\text{Capital employed}} \times 100$$

$$= \frac{60 + 15}{900} \text{ (as (3) above)} \times 100 = 8.34\%$$

8. Average collection period:

$$\frac{\text{Average debtors}}{\text{Sales}} = \frac{60 + 110}{2} = \frac{85}{500} \times 365 = 62 \text{ days}$$

9. Average credit period taken:

$$\frac{\text{Average creditors}}{\text{Purchases}} = \frac{35 + 65}{2} = \frac{50}{300} \times 365 = 61 \text{ days}$$

10. Rate of stock turnover:

$$\text{Average stock} = \frac{40 + 50}{2} = 45 \qquad \frac{500}{45} = 11.12 \text{ times}$$

11. Sales to fixed assets:

$$\frac{500}{820} = 0.61$$

The manufacturing fixed assets were not available. To have used them rather than the total of all fixed assets would have provided us with a better indication of plant utilization.

12. The gearing:

$$\frac{\text{Debentures}}{\text{Capital employed}} = \frac{150}{900} \times 100 = 16.67\%$$

shows that 16.67% of the assets were financed from long-term sources, other than equity.

13. Interest cover:

$$\frac{\text{Net profit before tax} + \text{interest}}{\text{Interest}} = \frac{60 + 15}{15} = 5 \text{ times}$$

The reasons why we could not compute certain investment ratios are as follows:

- The market price of the ordinary shares was not given.
- The net profit after tax was not given.
- The paid/proposed ordinary dividend for the year was not given.

Value added statements and ratios

Value added statements show how the value added (the wealth created), i.e. sales less materials and services bought from outside suppliers, is distributed between the stakeholders. The stakeholders of a company are the employees, the providers of capital, the government, and the company itself by means of depreciation and retained earnings.

Ratios can be computed using value added to measure the productivity of labour, capital and fixed assets and also the growth of the original inputs.

Summary: assessing the financial performance

The ratios

The ratios which are used to review a company's financial performance cover profitability, liquidity, efficiency, capital structure, employees and investment. Information can be used in the following ways:

☐ When you look at comparative figures for example, this year compared to last year, or company A compared to company B, it is useful to make working notes on each ratio/group of ratios to explain the variances and to highlight strengths and weaknesses, etc.

☐ If a ratio analysis is to be useful, it needs to be based on several years' figures so that trends can be identified and emerging problems detected.

☐ The quest for a 'yardstick', i.e. something against which performance can be measured, can be partly solved by using industry figures.

Limitations

Ratio analysis does have limitations, the principal ones being:

☐ The inadequacy of the source data, i.e. the final accounts, for example concerning the application of concepts and accounting policies, 'off-balance-sheet financing', etc.

☐ The way in which the ratios are computed: for example, the treatment of the bank overdraft as a long- or short-term source of finance; using the sales figure when purchases or cost of sales figures would be more appropriate; the profit figure could be one of many, for example net profit before tax, net profit after tax, etc.; the way in which the average debtors, creditors and stock are arrived at, i.e. taking no account of what happens during the intervening period.

☐ The terminology can also be very confusing.

If you have to carry out an interfirm comparison, beware! You cannot just compare with another firm in the same industrial sector. You also need to try to select companies which have some of the following characteristics:

☐ Have a similar product range.
☐ Are of a similar size.
☐ Have the same year-end.
☐ Use similar accounting policies.
☐ Finance their assets in a similar manner, i.e. the extent to which they use 'off-balance-sheet financing'.
☐ Have revalued their buildings around the same date.
☐ Are located in an area where overhead costs are similar.

Further reading

Berry, A., *Financial Accounting, An Introduction*, International Thomson Business Press, 1999.

Holmes, G. and Sugden, A., *Interpreting Company Reports and Accounts*, Financial Times Prentice Hall, 2000.

McKenzie, W., *The Financial Times Guide To: Using and Interpreting Company Accounts*, Financial Times Prentice Hall, 1998.

Pendlebury, M. and Groves, R., *Company Accounts, Analysis, Interpretation and Understanding*, International Thomson Business Press, 2000.

Other useful resources are:

- ☐ *UK Industrial Performance Analysis* (published annually, ICC Business Publications Ltd).
- ☐ Extel Cards.
- ☐ The Company Reports Section of a library, e.g. covering *The Times'* 1,000 companies.
- ☐ On the computer, *Micro View* by Extel and *Micro Extat*, as used by leading business schools.
- ☐ *Financial Analysis Made Easy* (CD Rom Publishing Co., 1995).
- ☐ Internet sources.

Suggested answers to self-assessment questions

Self-assessment 4.1: Throngfirth Manufacturing

See Table A.1.1 for answer to Question 1.
See Table A.1.2 for answers to Questions 2 and 3.

Points to note (not part of the answer)

Relating to Tables A.1.1 and A.1.2.

☐ First, notice that we have lumped together those overheads which are shared out according to the same method of apportionment, e.g. buildings insurance and lighting are both shared out according to floor area.

☐ The total column provides a cross-add which acts as a check on the arithmetic accuracy of the figures.

☐ We have used the word 'allocate' to mean an overhead which can be directly associated with a department/cost centre, and 'apportionment' to denote those overheads which cannot be identified with a specific department/cost centre. You should note that other authors do not attempt to draw such a fine distinction between these words.

☐ Also, even though we know the direct labour hours for the machine department, we do not use them to work out the overhead absorption rate. Why? Because the machine department overheads are being recovered using a rate per machine hour.

☐ Again, note that we use the 15 machine hours to compute the machine department overheads applicable to product PQ.

☐ Finally, when you select a basis of apportionment, e.g. floor area, you have to select the basis which is most appropriate for sharing out the particular item of overhead expenditure concerned.

Table A.1.1 Throngfirth Manufacturing: departmental overhead summary/analysis

Overheads	Total £	Production departments			Service departments	
		Machine £	Paint £	Assembly £	Stores £	Power £
Indirect materials & labour (allocated)	91,700	36,730	11,270	11,900	16,680	15,120
Fuel (allocated)	74,000	–	–	–	–	74,000
Buildings insurance & lighting (floor area)	9,600	4,800 ($^8/_{16}$)	1,200 ($^2/_{16}$)	2,400 ($^4/_{16}$)	600 ($^1/_{16}$)	600 ($^1/_{16}$)
Supervision & canteen (No. of employees)	43,200	12,960 ($^6/_{20}$)	4,320 ($^2/_{20}$)	17,280 ($^8/_{20}$)	4,320 ($^2/_{20}$)	4,320 ($^2/_{20}$)
Machinery insurance (value of machines)	4,800	2,880 ($^3/_5$)	960 ($^1/_5$)	–	–	960 ($^1/_5$)
Depreciation (allocated)	25,700	12,400	6,300	2,100	1,400	3,500
	249,000	69,770	24,050	33,680	23,000	98,500
Stores (technical estimates)		5,750	5,750	9,200	–23,000	2,300
						100,800
Power (technical estimates)		60,480	25,200	15,120		–100,800
	£249,000	£136,000	£55,000	£58,000		
Overhead absorption rates						
Machine hours		20,000 = £6.80				
Direct labour hours			5,000 = £11.00	8,000 = £7.25		

Table A.1.2 Throngfirth Manufacturing: calculation of the proposed selling price of product PQ

		£	£
Direct materials			1,277
Direct labour			
(4 hrs × £9)	Machine dept	36	
(3 hrs × £8)	Paint dept	24	
(16 hrs × £7)	Assembly dept	<u>112</u>	172
Overheads			
(15 hrs × £6.80)	Machine dept	102	
(3 hrs × £11)	Paint dept	33	
(16 hrs × £7.25)	Assembly dept	<u>116</u>	<u>251</u>
	Product cost		1,700
add Mark-up (40% × £1,700) =			680
	Proposed selling price		<u>2,380</u>

Self-assessment 5.2: Pawilkes & Co. Ltd

Activity cost pools

Dept 1 (£000)	Dept 2 (£000)	Setting-up (£000)	Computing (£000)	Purchasing (£000)	Total (£000)
680	410	40	200	100	<u>1430</u>
Cost drivers (000)					
340	410	10	40	50	
Machine hrs	Direct lab. hrs	Set-ups	Computer hrs	Orders	
£2 per machine hour	£1 per direct lab. hr	£4 per set-up	£5 per computer hour	£2 per order	

Activity-based costing profit statement

	Product D		Product E	
Sales/production (units) (£000)	200,000		120,000	
	£	£	£	£
Sales		2,400		3,360
Less prime cost		1,600		2,160
		800		1,200
Cost pools:				
Dept. 1 @ £2 per machine hour	200		480	
Dept. 2 @ £1 per direct lab. hour	50		360	
Setting up @ £4 per set-up	24		16	
Computing @ £5 per computer hour	100		100	
Purchasing @ £2 per order	80	454	20	976
Profit		346		224

Total profit = £570,000

Self-assessment 6.1: Heaton Postex plc

See Table A.1.3 for the answer to Question 1.

See Table A.1.4 for Question 2.

The contribution needed to produce a profit of £796 in Table A.1.3 would be as shown in Table A.1.5 (Question 3).

The answer to Question 4 is in Table A.1.6.

Table A.1.3 Heaton Postex plc: marginal costing statement

	Current position 20X8 Per unit £	40,000 units £000	Next year 20X9 Per unit £	50,000 units £000
Selling price	120	4,800	125	6,250
less variable cost	96	3,840	100	5,000
Contribution	24	960	25(20%)	1,250
(Proof £24 × 40,000)			(proof £25 × 50,000)	
less Fixed costs		164		186
Profit		796		1,064

Table A.1.4 Heaton Postex plc: breakeven points

	20X8 £000		20X9 £000
Fixed costs	164		186
Profit volume ratio (as above)	20%		20%
Breakeven point	£000		£000
(Fixed cost ÷ PV ratio) =	820	=	930

Table A.1.5 Heaton Postex plc: sales needed to achieve profit target

	£000
Fixed costs 20X9	186
add Profit	796
Contribution required	982

The number of units which must be sold to produce the contribution required is therefore

$$\frac{\text{contribution required}}{\text{contribution per unit}} = \frac{£982,000}{£25} = 39,280 \text{ units}$$

£000

This has a sales value of 39,280 units × £125 = 4,910 (Question 3)

Table A.1.6 Heaton Postex plc: amount available for additional fixed costs

		£000
The total contribution from the sale of 56,000 units @ £25 per unit would be		1,400
	£000	
less Fixed costs	186	
Profit target	1,200	1,386
Amount available for additional fixed costs		14

Points to note (not part of the answer)

Relating to Tables A.1.3 to A.1.6 inclusive.

☐ Good layout and presentation should make the information produced more under-standable.

☐ The contributions in (1) of £960,000 and £1,250,000 and (4) of £1,400,000 could be calculated quickly by multiplying the units sold by the contribution per unit.

☐ The profit volume ratio, i.e. the contribution as a percentage of sales, can be used to calculate the breakeven point. However, other methods are quite acceptable.

- [ ] Both parts (3) and (4) involve the use of the technique designed to help with profit target problems, i.e. the knowledge that the contribution required equals the fixed costs plus the profit target.
- [ ] In (4) a comparison is made between the contribution which is expected to be generated and the contribution which is needed to cover fixed costs and the profit target, the difference being the amount which is available to spend on additional fixed costs.

Self-assessment 6.2: Scoubado Manufacturing

See Tables A.1.7 and A.1.8.

The ranking in terms of the highest contribution per hour is:

1. L up to 60 units £60.
2. J up to 30 units £50.
3. J over 30 units £44.
4. K up to 24 units £32.
5. L over 60 units £30.
6. K over 24 units £28.

The maximum contribution per day is as shown in Table A.1.9.

Points to note (not part of the answer)

- [ ] The reductions in the selling prices for J, K and L respectively are matched by a reduction in their contribution per unit of the same amount.
- [ ] The key factor (limiting factor) in this problem was the productive time available.
- [ ] The above solution therefore answered the question, 'Which combination of products will maximize the contribution per day if there are only 42 hours of production time available?'

Table A.1.7 Scoubado Manufacturing: marginal costing/limiting factor analysis (first output level)

Output level (first)	J up to 30 units £	K up to 24 units £	L up to 60 units £
Selling price	75	108	59
less Variable cost	50	84	39
Contribution	25	24	20
Production per hour (units)	×	×	×
	2	1.33	3
	=	=	=
Contribution per hour	£50	£32	£60

Table A.1.8 Scoubado Manufacturing: marginal costing/limiting factor analysis (second output level)

		J over 30 units £	K over 24 units £	L over 60 units £
	Selling price	72	105	49
less	Variable cost	50	84	39
	Contribution	£22	£21	£10
Production per hour (units)		× 2	× 1.33	× 3
		=	=	=
	Contribution per hour	£44	£28	£30

Table A.1.9 Scoubado Manufacturing: maximum contribution per day

Product	Quantity	Time per unit	Total time (hours)	Contribution per hour	Total
	units	mins		£	£
L	60	20	20	60	1,200
J	30	30	15	50	750
			35		
J	14	30	7	44	308
			42 hours		2,258

☐ When the total hours needed reached 35 hours, the final question which had to be answered was, 'With the seven hours left and using the third ranked contribution, how many units can be produced?' (Seven hours at half an hour per unit = 14 units.)

Self-assessment 6.3: Holme Honley Products plc

The breakeven chart (Question 1) is shown in Figure A.1.1, which also indicates the margin of safety. Table A.1.10 answers Question 2.

Points to note (not part of the answer)

☐ The horizontal scale of the breakeven chart can be expressed in terms of output or level of activity.

☐ The breakeven point can be worked out mathematically, in terms of value and output/ level of activity.

☐ To read off the position for a particular level of activity from the breakeven chart, all you have to do is project a vertical line upwards (e.g. at 60%) to see where it crosses the fixed cost line, the total cost line and the sales line. The gap between the £1,800 total cost and the sales revenue of £1,500 represents the loss of £300.

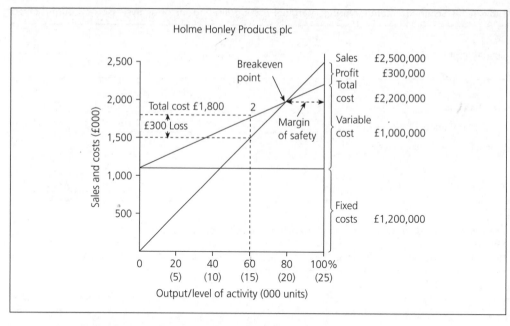

Figure A.1.1 Holme Honley Products plc: breakeven chart

Table A.1.10 Holme Honley Products plc: calculation of the breakeven point

	Per unit £		25,000 units £000	15,000 units £000
Selling price	100		2,500	1,500
less Variable cost	40		1,000	600
Contribution	60	(60% PV ratio)	1,500	900
less Fixed costs			1,200	1,200
Profit			300	(Loss) (300)

Breakeven point (£000)

= fixed cost ÷ PV ratio

$$= £1,200 \times \frac{100}{60} = £2,000$$

Breakeven point (in 000 units)

$$= \frac{\text{fixed cost}}{\text{contribution per unit}} = \frac{£1,200}{£60} = 20$$

Self-assessment 7.1: Budgetary control self-check

Budget

A budget has been defined by the CIMA (The Chartered Institute of Management Accountants) as:

> A plan expressed in money. It is prepared and approved prior to the budget period and may show income, expenditure, and the capital to be employed. May be drawn up showing incremental effects on former budgeted or actual figures, or be compiled by zero base budgeting.

Additional notes

You should note that a budget can be prepared in terms of quantity and/or value. For example, in practice, the production budget will first of all be drawn up in terms of quantity only. When it is clear that it coheres with the other budgets, e.g. sales, material requirements, labour requirements, etc., it will then be costed.

The keywords which you could have included in your own definition could include the following:

☐ It needs to be *predetermined/prepared in advance* of the period to which it relates.
☐ It aims at achieving specific *objectives*.
☐ It lays down the *policy* to be followed so that the objectives can be attained.
☐ In addition to budgeting income and expenditure it can also be used to budget the capital employed.

Budgetary control

Budgetary control has been defined by CIMA as:

> The establishment of budgets relating the responsibilities of executives to the requirements of a policy, and by continuous comparison of actual with budgeted results, either to secure by individual action the objectives of that policy or to provide a basis for its revision.

Additional notes

The keywords which you should have included in your definition are as follows:

☐ *Control by responsibility*.
☐ The *policy* to be followed.
☐ The *continuous comparison* of actual/budgeted figures, i.e. monitor at frequent intervals.
☐ *Management action* relating to the significant adverse variances, i.e. *management by exception*.
☐ The *attainment of the objectives*.
☐ The *revision* of the budget, if necessary, e.g. where basic assumptions change.

For both budgets and budgetary control you could also include:

☐ The involvement/participation of certain employees, e.g. supervisors.
☐ A common-sense approach, e.g. the setting of realistic and attainable targets.
☐ Consideration of the interrelationships between budgets.
☐ The importance of taking behavioural factors into account.

The principal budget factor

The principal budget factor (also known as the 'key factor' or 'limiting factor') is the factor which must be taken into account first when budgeting, because it places a constraint upon the activities of a company/organization. For example, if production capacity was limited in a certain period to 45,000 units it would be stupid to have a sales budget of 75,000 units. You cannot sell what you have not got! However, the principal budget factor (key factor/limiting factor) is not a fixed state of affairs and managers can, by their actions, eliminate it or reduce its effect. For example, if production capacity was the limiting factor, it could be increased by working shifts, buying more machines, using subcontractors, etc.

Control by responsibility

Control by responsibility in budgeting takes place when the responsibility for a budget/ part of a budget is **delegated** to a particular person who then becomes responsible for the achievement of the targets set. He or she has to explain to management the reasons why targets are not being achieved and the reasons for significant adverse variances. For example, a sales area manager will be responsible for the achievement of monthly sales targets in his/her area. In turn, each individual sales person would be responsible for their own monthly sales target.

Management by exception

This is a system which is designed to enable managers to use their time in a more productive/effective way. Reports and statements should highlight those items of significance which are *not* going according to plan. Managers will, therefore, devote a lot of time and effort into carefully reviewing such items and putting into place any necessary corrective action. They can devote their time and talents to those tasks which really need their undivided attention. It in effect directs and in some ways forces managers to manage!

Self-assessment 7.2: The difference between profit and cash

The cash budget deals only with the actual cash which comes in or goes out during the period, i.e. the actual physical movement of cash. However, the profit and loss account deals with items which are not included in the cash budget, which in the case of Brendug Co. Ltd are as follows:

☐ The sales figure of £88,000 represents the total sales made during the period irrespective of whether or not the cash has been received.
☐ £66,000 is the total purchases figure for the period, i.e. it includes those which have been paid for in cash of £54,000 and those which have not yet been paid for of £12,000.
☐ The closing stock of materials of £6,000. This is deducted in computing the cost of sales but does not affect the cash budget at all.
☐ The charge for the use of plant and machinery, i.e. depreciation, charges a proportion of the cost in computing the loss.

Other comments

It must also be remembered that when profit is generated it is used to finance the purchase of fixed assets such as plant and machinery, fixtures and fittings, and to finance increases in the working capital, e.g. stocks and debtors. Thus, profit does not tend to stay cash for long, because the business spends it. Accrued and prepaid items will also be adjusted for in the profit and loss account but will not be adjusted for in the cash budget.

Self-assessment 7.3: Jeanles Ltd

See Tables A.1.11–A.1.13.

Table A.1.11 Jeanles Ltd: cash budget

	Inflows			Outflows				
	Opening balance	Sales	Purchases	Rent	Wages & salaries	General expenses	Fixed assets	Closing balance
	£000	£000	£000	£000	£000	£000	£000	£000
Jan	60 Share capital	–	–	1.4	1	0.5	59	(1.9)
Feb	(1.9)	8	–		1	0.5		4.6
Mar	4.6	20	10		1	0.5	16	(2.9)
Apr	(2.9)	28	15	1.4	1	0.5		7.2
May	7.2	28	21		1	0.5		12.7
Jun	12.7	28	21		1	0.5		18.2
		112	67	2.8	6.0	3.0	75	
+ debtors (1 month)		28						
		140						
+ creditors (2 months)			42					
			109					

Table A.1.12 Jeanles Ltd: budgeted profit and loss account

		£000	£000
	Sales		140
less	Cost of sales:		
	Opening stock	–	
add	Purchases	109	
		109	
less	Closing stock	4	105
	Gross profit (25% of sales)		35
less	Expenses:		
	Rent	2.8	
	Wages and salaries	6.0	
	General expenses	3.0	
	Depreciation (75 × 20%) for half-year	7.5	19.3
	Net profit		15.7

Table A.1.13 Jeanles Ltd: budgeted balance sheet

		£000	£000
	Capital employed:		
	Issued ordinary share capital	60	
	Retained profit	15.7	75.7
	Employment of capital:		
	Fixed assets	75	
less	Depreciation	7.5	67.5
	Working capital:		
	Current assets		
	Stock	4	
	Debtors (one month)	28	
	Cash & bank (per cash budget)	18.2	
		50.2	
	Current liabilities:		
	Creditors (two months)	42	8.2
			75.7

Comments (not part of the answer)

Note that during January and March the cash budget reveals an overdraft but this is covered by the current overdraft limit negotiated with the bank. Note also that the depreciation of £7,500 is for half a year. It was assumed that all the cash from the issue of the ordinary share capital would be received before January 20X4. Note also that the internal balance sheet format used started with the capital employed, it could have used the format which we used in Table 7.10 on page 65.

Self-assessment 8.1: Material variances

Material cost variance

This represents the difference between the actual cost of materials, £48,100, and the standard cost of the materials (for the actual level of activity, i.e. 8,000 units) of £48,000. Because the actual cost exceeded the standard cost by £100, this is an overspend, and classified as an adverse variance.

Material price variance

This is that part of the material cost variance which arises from paying an actual price for materials of £1.85 per kilo, which is different from the standard price of £2 per kilo which it was planned to pay. In the example used the difference of 15p per kilo less than standard represents a cost saving and is, therefore, classed as a favourable variance.

The price variance can also be calculated as shown in Table A.1.14.

This is really saying that for every kilo of material used a price saving of 15p takes place.

Also note in the example that the figures used of £48,100 and £52,000 both use the same quantity, i.e. the actual quantity of 26,000 kilos. Only the prices are different, i.e. £1.85 per kilo and £2 per kilo.

Table A.1.14 The material price variance

	Standard price per kilo	£2.00
less	Actual price per kilo	£1.85
	Saving per kilo	£0.15

Actual materials used × price saving = £3,900 (favourable)
(26,000 kilos)   (15p)

Material usage variance

That part of the material cost variance which results from using an actual quantity of materials which is different from the standard quantity of materials applicable to the actual level of activity/output. We can compute the usage variance as shown in Table A.1.15.

Table A.1.15 The material usage variance

		kilos
	Standard quantity (for actual level of output) of materials	24,000
less	Actual quantity of materials used	26,000
	Excess usage	(2,000)

Excess usage × standard price = usage variance = £4,000
(2,000 kilos)   (£2)   (adverse)

Thus, this variance has arisen because it takes more material than planned to produce the 8,000 units. Also note in our example that both calculations use the same price figure, i.e. the standard price; only the quantities are different, i.e. 24,000 kilos standard and 26,000 kilos actual. The adverse usage variance could have been caused by buying a lower-quality material at the lower price of £1.85 per kilo. Thus, a favourable price variance could account and help explain an adverse usage variance.

Self-assessment 8.2: Labour variances

Work sheet

See Table A.1.16.

Further proof of the two subvariances are:

labour rate variance = (actual hours × rate increase)
$$(1950 \times 50p) = £975 \text{ (adverse)}$$

It is adverse, because the labour rate which was actually paid was 50p per hour more than the planned rate.

labour efficiency variance = actual hours less standard hours
$$(1,950) \qquad (2,000)$$
$$= 50 \text{ hours @ standard rate } (£8)$$
$$= £400 \text{ favourable}$$

This variance is favourable because the actual time taken to do the work was less than the standard time allowed. From a study of the answer, it can be observed that the labour cost variance (sometimes called the 'wages cost variance') is the difference between the actual hours spent producing the actual production of 1,000 units at the actual labour rate per hour, and the standard labour time allowed to produce (the actual production) 1,000 units at the standard labour rate per hour.

Table A.1.16 Standard costing: labour variance

	Labour cost variance £	Labour rate variance £	Labour efficiency variance £
Actual hours @ actual rate			
(1,950 @ £8.50)	16,575	16,575	–
Standard hours @ standard rate			
(2,000 @ £8)	16,000	–	16,000
Actual hours @ standard rate			
(1,950 @ £8)		15,600	15,600
	–	15,600	15,600
	575	975	400
	(Adverse)	(Adverse)	(Favourable)

Summary (proof)		£
Labour rate variance	(Adverse)	(975)
Labour efficiency variance	Favourable	400
= Labour cost variance	(Adverse)	(575)

Table A.1.17 The equivalent cash price via present value tables

	£
Payable on delivery (i.e. now)	3,000
The present value of an annuity of £3,000 for 3 years @ 12% (£3,000 × 2.402) (Table 9.9)	7,206
The present value of £5,000 in 4 years' time (£5,000 × 0.636) (Table 9.8)	3,180
The present value of £2,500 in 5 years' time (£2,500 × 0.567) (Table 9.8)	1,417.5
Equivalent cash price	14,803.5

Self-assessment 9.1: The equivalent cash price

See Table A.1.17.

This represents the present value of the cash which will be paid out now and in the future. It also indicates the amount which would have to be invested now at 12% compound interest per annum to produce the instalments as and when they are needed, i.e. £14,803.5 less the delivery payment of £3,000 will have to be invested at the outset. This would then produce £3,000 × 3 years = £9,000 plus £5,000 at the end of the fourth year and £2,500 at the end of the fifth year, a total of £16,500 (excluding the delivery payment).

Self-assessment 9.2: Identical cash flows/the treatment of depreciation

The NPV is negative, i.e. the discounted cash flows come to less than the initial investment; the project should not, therefore, go ahead (see Table A.1.18).

Table A.1.18 Identical cash flows/the treatment of depreciation

Annual cash flow £	Present value of an annuity of £1 for 6 years @ 16%*	Present value of cash flows £
12,000 ×	3.685 =	44,220
less Initial investment		60,000
Net present value		(15,780)

* As per Table 9.9.

Note on depreciation

Depreciation is irrelevant: as it had not been deducted in computing the cash flows, no adjustment to the cash flows was necessary.

Self-assessment 9.3: Becwik Ltd

See Table A.1.19.

The project has an NPV of £6,940 positive and is, therefore, worthy of consideration, i.e. it is acceptable according to the financial criteria. But non-financial considerations also need to be investigated. Note that the depreciation had not been deducted in computing the incremental cash flow and is therefore irrelevant.

Table A.1.19 Becwik Ltd: net present value

Year	Cash flow £000	Discount factor 14%	Present value £000
1	10	0.877	8.77
2	20	0.769	15.38
3	40	0.675	27.00
4	50	0.592	29.60
5	10	0.519	5.19
			85.94
		less Initial cost	79.00
		Net present value	**6.94**

APPENDIX 2

Present value tables and annuity tables

Table A.2.1 Present value of £1 due at end of n years

n	1%	2%	3%	4%	5%	6%	7%	8%	9%	10%	n
1	0.99010	0.98039	0.97007	0.96154	0.95238	0.94340	0.93458	0.92593	0.91743	0.90909	1
2	0.98030	0.96117	0.94260	0.92456	0.90703	0.89000	0.87344	0.85734	0.84168	0.82645	2
3	0.97059	0.94232	0.91514	0.88900	0.86384	0.83962	0.81630	0.79383	0.77218	0.75131	3
4	0.96098	0.92385	0.88849	0.85480	0.82270	0.79209	0.76290	0.73503	0.70843	0.68301	4
5	0.95147	0.90573	0.86261	0.82193	0.78353	0.74726	0.71299	0.68058	0.64993	0.62092	5
6	0.94204	0.88797	0.83748	0.79031	0.74622	0.70496	0.66634	0.63017	0.59627	0.56447	6
7	0.93272	0.87056	0.81309	0.75992	0.71068	0.66506	0.62275	0.58349	0.54703	0.51316	7
8	0.92348	0.85349	0.78941	0.73069	0.67684	0.62741	0.58201	0.54027	0.50187	0.46651	8
9	0.91434	0.83675	0.76642	0.70259	0.64461	0.59190	0.54393	0.50025	0.46043	0.42410	9
10	0.90529	0.82035	0.74409	0.67556	0.61391	0.55839	0.50835	0.46319	0.42241	0.38554	10
11	0.89632	0.80426	0.72242	0.64958	0.58468	0.52679	0.47509	0.42888	0.38753	0.35049	11
12	0.88745	0.78849	0.70138	0.62460	0.55684	0.49697	0.44401	0.39711	0.35553	0.31863	12
13	0.87866	0.77303	0.68095	0.60057	0.53032	0.46884	0.41496	0.36770	0.32618	0.28966	13
14	0.86996	0.75787	0.66112	0.57747	0.50507	0.44230	0.38782	0.34046	0.29925	0.26333	14
15	0.86135	0.74301	0.64186	0.55526	0.48102	0.41726	0.36245	0.31524	0.27454	0.23939	15
16	0.85282	0.72845	0.62317	0.53391	0.45811	0.39365	0.33873	0.29189	0.25187	0.21763	16
17	0.84438	0.71416	0.60502	0.51337	0.43630	0.37136	0.31657	0.27027	0.23107	0.19784	17
18	0.83602	0.70016	0.58739	0.49363	0.41552	0.35034	0.29586	0.25025	0.21199	0.17986	18
19	0.82774	0.68643	0.57029	0.47464	0.39573	0.33051	0.27651	0.23171	0.19449	0.16351	19
20	0.81954	0.67297	0.55367	0.45639	0.37689	0.31180	0.25842	0.21455	0.17843	0.14864	20
21	0.81143	0.65978	0.53755	0.43883	0.35894	0.29415	0.24151	0.19866	0.16370	0.13513	21
22	0.80340	0.64684	0.52189	0.42195	0.34185	0.27750	0.22571	0.18394	0.15018	0.12285	22
23	0.79544	0.63414	0.50669	0.40573	0.32557	0.26180	0.21095	0.17031	0.13778	0.11168	23
24	0.78757	0.62172	0.49193	0.39012	0.31007	0.24698	0.19715	0.15770	0.12640	0.10153	24
25	0.77977	0.60953	0.47760	0.37512	0.29530	0.23300	0.18425	0.14602	0.11597	0.09230	25

Note: $PV = £1/(1 + r)^n$

Table A.2.1 continued

n	11%	12%	13%	14%	15%	16%	17%	18%	19%	20%	n
1	0.90090	0.89286	0.88496	0.87719	0.86957	0.86207	0.85470	0.84746	0.84034	0.83333	1
2	0.81162	0.79719	0.78315	0.76947	0.75614	0.74316	0.73051	0.71818	0.70616	0.69444	2
3	0.73119	0.71178	0.69305	0.67497	0.65752	0.64066	0.62437	0.60863	0.59342	0.57870	3
4	0.65873	0.63552	0.61332	0.59208	0.57175	0.55229	0.53365	0.51579	0.49867	0.48225	4
5	0.59345	0.56743	0.54276	0.51937	0.49718	0.47611	0.45611	0.43711	0.41905	0.40188	5
6	0.53464	0.50663	0.48032	0.45559	0.43233	0.41044	0.38984	0.37043	0.35214	0.33490	6
7	0.48166	0.45235	0.42506	0.39964	0.37594	0.35383	0.33320	0.31392	0.29592	0.27908	7
8	0.43393	0.40388	0.37616	0.35056	0.32690	0.30503	0.28487	0.26604	0.24592	0.23257	8
9	0.39092	0.36061	0.33288	0.30751	0.28426	0.26295	0.24340	0.22546	0.20897	0.19381	9
10	0.35218	0.32197	0.29459	0.26974	0.24718	0.22668	0.20804	0.19106	0.17560	0.16151	10
11	0.31728	0.28748	0.26070	0.23662	0.21494	0.19542	0.17781	0.16192	0.14756	0.13459	11
12	0.28584	0.25667	0.23071	0.20756	0.18691	0.16846	0.15197	0.13722	0.12400	0.11216	12
13	0.25751	0.22917	0.20416	0.18207	0.16253	0.14523	0.12989	0.11629	0.10420	0.09346	13
14	0.23199	0.20462	0.18068	0.15971	0.14133	0.12520	0.11102	0.09855	0.08757	0.07789	14
15	0.20900	0.18270	0.15989	0.14010	0.12289	0.10793	0.09489	0.08352	0.07359	0.06491	15
16	0.18829	0.16312	0.14150	0.12289	0.10686	0.09304	0.08110	0.07078	0.06184	0.05409	16
17	0.16963	0.14564	0.12522	0.10780	0.09393	0.08021	0.06932	0.05998	0.05196	0.04507	17
18	0.15282	0.13004	0.11081	0.09456	0.08080	0.06914	0.05925	0.05083	0.04367	0.03756	18
19	0.13768	0.11611	0.09806	0.08295	0.07026	0.05961	0.05064	0.04308	0.03669	0.03130	19
20	0.12403	0.10367	0.08678	0.07276	0.06110	0.05139	0.04328	0.03651	0.03084	0.02608	20
21	0.11174	0.09256	0.07680	0.06383	0.05313	0.04430	0.03699	0.03094	0.02591	0.02174	21
22	0.10067	0.08264	0.06796	0.05599	0.04620	0.03819	0.03162	0.02622	0.02178	0.01811	22
23	0.09069	0.07379	0.06014	0.04911	0.04017	0.03292	0.02702	0.02222	0.01830	0.01509	23
24	0.08170	0.06588	0.05322	0.04308	0.03493	0.02838	0.02310	0.01883	0.01538	0.01258	24
25	0.07361	0.05882	0.04710	0.03779	0.03038	0.02447	0.01974	0.01596	0.01292	0.01048	25

Table A.2.1 continued

n	21%	22%	23%	24%	25%	26%	27%	28%	29%	30%	n
1	0.82645	0.81967	0.81301	0.80645	0.80000	0.79365	0.78740	0.78125	0.77519	0.76923	1
2	0.68301	0.67186	0.66098	0.65036	0.64000	0.62988	0.62000	0.61035	0.60093	0.59172	2
3	0.56447	0.55071	0.53738	0.52449	0.51200	0.49991	0.48819	0.47684	0.46583	0.45517	3
4	0.46651	0.45140	0.43690	0.42297	0.40960	0.39675	0.38440	0.37253	0.36111	0.35013	4
5	0.38554	0.37000	0.35520	0.34111	0.32768	0.31488	0.30268	0.29104	0.27993	0.26933	5
6	0.31863	0.30328	0.28878	0.27509	0.26214	0.24991	0.23833	0.22737	0.21700	0.20718	6
7	0.26333	0.24859	0.23478	0.22184	0.20972	0.19834	0.18766	0.17764	0.16822	0.15937	7
8	0.21763	0.20376	0.19088	0.17891	0.16777	0.15741	0.14776	0.13878	0.13040	0.12259	8
9	0.17986	0.16702	0.15519	0.14428	0.13422	0.12493	0.11635	0.10842	0.10109	0.09430	9
10	0.14864	0.13690	0.12617	0.11635	0.10737	0.09915	0.09161	0.08470	0.07836	0.07254	10
11	0.12285	0.11221	0.10258	0.09383	0.08590	0.07869	0.07214	0.06617	0.06075	0.05580	11
12	0.10153	0.09198	0.08339	0.07567	0.06872	0.06245	0.05680	0.05170	0.04709	0.04292	12
13	0.08391	0.07539	0.06780	0.06103	0.05498	0.04957	0.04472	0.04039	0.03650	0.03302	13
14	0.06934	0.06180	0.05512	0.04921	0.04398	0.03934	0.03522	0.03155	0.02830	0.02540	14
15	0.05731	0.05065	0.04481	0.03969	0.03518	0.03122	0.02773	0.02465	0.02194	0.01954	15
16	0.04736	0.04152	0.03643	0.03201	0.02815	0.02478	0.02183	0.01926	0.01700	0.01503	16
17	0.03914	0.03403	0.02962	0.02581	0.02252	0.01967	0.01719	0.01505	0.01318	0.01156	17
18	0.03235	0.02789	0.02408	0.02082	0.01801	0.01561	0.01354	0.01175	0.01022	0.00889	18
19	0.02673	0.02286	0.01958	0.01679	0.01441	0.01239	0.01066	0.00918	0.00792	0.00684	19
20	0.02209	0.01874	0.01592	0.01354	0.01153	0.00983	0.00839	0.00717	0.00614	0.00526	20
21	0.01826	0.01536	0.01294	0.01092	0.00922	0.00780	0.00661	0.00561	0.00476	0.00405	21
22	0.01509	0.01259	0.01052	0.00880	0.00738	0.00619	0.00520	0.00438	0.00369	0.00311	22
23	0.01247	0.01032	0.00855	0.00710	0.00590	0.00491	0.00410	0.00342	0.00286	0.00239	23
24	0.01031	0.00846	0.00695	0.00573	0.00472	0.00390	0.00323	0.00267	0.00222	0.00184	24
25	0.00852	0.00693	0.00565	0.00462	0.00378	0.00310	0.00254	0.00209	0.00172	0.00152	25

Table A.2.1 continued

n	31%	32%	33%	34%	35%	36%	37%	38%	39%	40%	n
1	0.76336	0.75758	0.75188	0.74627	0.74074	0.73529	0.72993	0.72464	0.71942	0.71429	1
2	0.58272	0.57392	0.56532	0.55692	0.54870	0.54066	0.53279	0.52510	0.51757	0.51020	2
3	0.44482	0.43479	0.42505	0.41561	0.40644	0.39754	0.38890	0.38051	0.37235	0.36443	3
4	0.33956	0.32939	0.31959	0.31016	0.30107	0.29231	0.28387	0.27573	0.26788	0.26031	4
5	0.25920	0.24953	0.24029	0.23146	0.22301	0.21493	0.20720	0.19980	0.19272	0.18593	5
6	0.19787	0.18904	0.18067	0.17273	0.16520	0.15804	0.15124	0.14479	0.13865	0.13281	6
7	0.15104	0.14321	0.13584	0.12890	0.12237	0.11621	0.11040	0.10492	0.09975	0.09486	7
8	0.11530	0.10849	0.10214	0.09620	0.09064	0.08545	0.08058	0.07603	0.07176	0.06776	8
9	0.08802	0.08219	0.07680	0.07179	0.06714	0.06283	0.05882	0.05509	0.05163	0.04840	9
10	0.06719	0.06227	0.05774	0.05357	0.04973	0.04620	0.04293	0.03992	0.03714	0.03457	10
11	0.05129	0.04717	0.04341	0.03998	0.03684	0.03397	0.03134	0.02893	0.02672	0.02469	11
12	0.03915	0.03574	0.03264	0.02989	0.02729	0.02498	0.02287	0.02096	0.01922	0.01764	12
13	0.02989	0.02707	0.02454	0.02227	0.02021	0.01837	0.01670	0.01519	0.01383	0.01260	13
14	0.02281	0.02051	0.01845	0.01662	0.01497	0.01350	0.01219	0.01101	0.00995	0.00900	14
15	0.01742	0.01554	0.01387	0.01240	0.01109	0.00993	0.00890	0.00798	0.00716	0.00643	15
16	0.01329	0.01177	0.01043	0.00925	0.00822	0.00730	0.00649	0.00578	0.00515	0.00459	16
17	0.01015	0.00892	0.00784	0.00691	0.00609	0.00537	0.00474	0.00419	0.00370	0.00328	17
18	0.00775	0.00676	0.00590	0.00515	0.00451	0.00395	0.00346	0.00304	0.00267	0.00234	18
19	0.00591	0.00512	0.00443	0.00385	0.00334	0.00290	0.00253	0.00220	0.00192	0.00167	19
20	0.00451	0.00388	0.00333	0.00287	0.00247	0.00213	0.00184	0.00159	0.00138	0.00120	20
21	0.00345	0.00294	0.00251	0.00214	0.00183	0.00157	0.00135	0.00115	0.00099	0.00085	21
22	0.00263	0.00223	0.00188	0.00160	0.00136	0.00115	0.00098	0.00084	0.00071	0.00061	22
23	0.00201	0.00169	0.00142	0.00119	0.00101	0300085	0.00072	0.00061	0.00051	0.00044	23
24	0.00153	0.00128	0.00107	0.00089	0.00074	0.00062	0.00052	0.00044	0.00037	0.00031	24
25	0.00117	0.00097	0.00080	0.00066	0.00055	0.00046	0.00038	0.00032	0.00027	0.00022	25

Table A.2.2 Present value of an annuity of £1 for n years

n	1%	2%	3%	4%	5%	6%	7%	8%	9%	10%	n
1	0.9901	0.9804	0.9709	0.9615	0.9524	0.9434	0.9346	0.9259	0.9174	0.9091	1
2	1.9704	1.9416	1.9135	1.8861	1.8594	1.8334	1.8080	1.7833	1.7591	1.7355	2
3	2.9410	2.8839	2.8286	2.7751	2.7232	2.6730	2.6243	2.5771	2.5313	2.4868	3
4	3.9020	3.8077	3.7171	3.6299	3.5459	3.4651	3.3872	3.3121	3.2397	3.1699	4
5	4.8535	4.7134	4.5797	4.4518	4.3295	4.2124	4.1002	3.9927	3.8896	3.7908	5
6	5.7955	5.6014	5.4172	5.2421	5.0757	4.9173	4.7665	4.6229	4.4859	4.3553	6
7	6.7282	6.4720	6.2302	6.0020	5.7863	5.5824	5.3893	5.2064	5.0329	4.8684	7
8	7.6517	7.3254	7.0196	6.7327	6.4632	6.2098	5.9713	5.7466	5.5348	5.3349	8
9	8.5661	8.1622	7.7861	7.4353	7.1078	6.8017	6.5152	6.2469	5.9852	5.7590	9
10	9.4714	8.9825	8.5302	8.1109	7.7217	7.3601	7.0236	6.7101	6.4176	6.1446	10
11	10.3677	9.7868	9.2526	8.7604	8.3064	7.8868	7.4987	7.1389	6.8052	6.4951	11
12	11.2552	10.5753	9.9539	9.3850	8.8632	8.3838	7.9427	7.5361	7.1607	6.8137	12
13	12.1338	11.3483	10.6349	9.9856	9.3935	8.8527	8.3576	7.9038	7.4869	7.1034	13
14	13.0038	12.1062	11.2960	10.5631	9.8986	9.2950	8.7454	8.2442	7.7861	7.3667	14
15	13.8651	12.8492	11.9379	11.1183	10.3796	9.7122	9.1079	8.5595	8.0607	7.6061	15
16	14.7180	13.5777	12.5610	11.6522	10.8377	10.1059	9.4466	8.8514	8.3125	7.8237	16
17	15.5624	14.2918	13.1660	12.1656	11.2740	10.4772	9.7632	9.1216	8.5436	8.0215	17
18	16.3984	14.9920	13.7534	12.6592	11.6895	10.8276	10.0591	9.3719	8.7556	8.2014	18
19	17.2261	15.6784	14.3237	13.1339	12.0853	11.1581	10.3356	9.6036	8.9501	8.3649	19
20	18.0457	16.3514	14.8774	13.5903	12.4622	11.4699	10.5940	9.8181	9.1285	8.5136	20
21	18.8571	17.0111	15.4149	14.0291	12.8211	11.7640	10.8355	10.0168	9.2922	8.6487	21
22	19.6605	17.6580	15.9368	14.4511	13.1630	12.0416	11.0612	10.2007	9.4424	8.7715	22
23	20.4559	18.2921	16.4435	14.8568	13.4885	12.3033	11.2722	10.3710	9.5802	8.8832	23
24	21.2435	18.9139	16.9355	15.2469	13.7986	12.5503	11.4693	10.5287	9.7066	8.9847	24
25	22.0233	19.5234	17.4131	15.6220	14.0939	12.7833	11.6536	10.6748	9.8226	9.0770	25

Table A.2.2 continued

n	11%	12%	13%	14%	15%	16%	17%	18%	19%	20%	n
1	0.0009	0.8929	0.8850	0.3772	0.8696	0.8621	0.8547	0.8475	0.8403	0.8333	1
2	1.7125	1.6901	1.6681	1.6467	1.6257	1.6052	1.5852	1.5656	1.5465	1.5278	2
3	2.4437	2.4018	2.3612	2.3216	2.2832	2.2459	2.2096	2.1743	2.1399	2.1065	3
4	3.1024	3.0373	2.9745	2.9137	2.8550	2.7982	2.7432	2.6901	2.6386	2.5887	4
5	3.6959	3.6048	3.5172	3.4331	3.3522	3.2743	3.1993	3.1272	3.0576	2.9906	5
6	4.2305	4.1114	3.9976	3.8887	3.7845	3.6847	3.5892	3.4976	3.4098	3.3255	6
7	4.7122	4.5638	4.4226	4.2883	4.1604	4.0386	3.9224	3.8115	3.7057	3.6046	7
8	5.1461	4.9676	4.7988	4.6389	4.4873	4.3436	4.2072	4.0776	3.9544	3.8372	8
9	5.5370	5.3282	5.1317	4.9464	4.7716	4.6065	4.4506	4.3030	4.1633	4.0310	9
10	5.8892	5.6502	5.4262	5.2161	5.0188	4.8332	4.6586	4.4941	4.3389	4.1925	10
11	6.2065	5.9377	5.6869	5.4527	5.2337	5.0286	4.8364	4.6560	4.4865	4.3271	11
12	6.4924	6.1944	5.9176	5.6603	5.4206	5.1971	4.9884	4.7932	4.6105	4.4392	12
13	6.7499	6.4235	6.1218	5.8424	5.5931	5.3423	5.1183	4.9095	4.7147	4.5327	13
14	6.9819	6.6282	6.3025	6.0021	5.7245	5.4675	5.2293	5.0081	4.8023	4.6106	14
15	7.1909	6.8109	6.4624	6.1422	5.8474	5.5755	5.3242	5.0916	4.8759	4.6755	15
16	7.3792	6.9740	6.6039	6.2651	5.9542	5.6685	5.4053	5.1624	4.9377	4.7296	16
17	7.5488	7.1196	6.7291	6.3729	6.0472	5.7487	5.4746	5.2223	4.9897	4.7746	17
18	7.7016	7.2497	6.8399	6.4674	6.1280	5.8178	5.5339	5.2732	5.0333	4.8122	18
19	7.8393	7.3658	6.9380	6.5504	6.1982	5.8775	5.5845	5.3162	5.0700	4.8435	19
20	7.9633	7.4694	7.0248	6.6231	6.2593	5.9288	5.6278	5.3527	5.1009	4.8696	20
21	8.0751	7.5620	7.1016	6.6870	6.3125	5.9731	5.6648	5.3837	5.1268	4.8913	21
22	8.1757	7.6446	7.1695	6.7429	6.3587	6.0113	5.6964	5.4099	5.1486	4.9094	22
23	8.2664	7.7184	7.2297	6.7921	6.3988	6.0442	5.7234	5.4321	5.1668	4.9245	23
24	8.3481	7.7843	7.2829	6.8351	6.4338	6.0726	5.7465	5.4509	5.1822	4.9371	24
25	8.4217	7.8431	7.3300	6.8729	6.4641	6.0971	5.7662	5.4669	5.1951	4.9476	25

Table A.2.2 continued

n	21%	22%	23%	24%	25%	26%	27%	28%	29%	30%	n
1	0.8264	0.8197	0.8130	0.8065	0.8000	0.7937	0.7874	0.7813	0.7752	0.7592	1
2	1.5095	1.4915	1.4740	1.4568	1.4400	1.4235	1.4074	1.3916	1.3761	1.3609	2
3	2.0738	2.0422	2.0114	1.9813	1.9520	1.9234	1.8956	1.8684	1.8420	1.8161	3
4	2.5404	2.4936	2.4483	2.4043	2.3616	2.3202	2.2800	2.2410	2.2031	2.1662	4
5	2.9260	2.8636	2.8035	2.7454	2.6893	2.6351	2.5827	2.5320	2.4830	2.4356	5
6	3.2446	3.1669	3.0923	3.0205	2.9514	2.8850	2.8210	2.7594	2.7000	2.6427	6
7	3.5079	3.4155	3.3270	3.2423	3.1611	3.0833	3.0087	2.9370	2.8682	2.8021	7
8	3.7256	3.6193	3.5179	3.4212	3.3289	3.2407	3.1564	3.0758	2.9986	2.9247	8
9	3.9054	3.7863	3.6731	3.5655	3.4631	3.3657	3.2728	3.1842	3.0997	3.0190	9
10	4.0541	3.9232	3.7993	3.6819	3.5705	3.4648	3.3644	3.2689	3.1781	3.0915	10
11	4.1769	4.0354	3.9018	3.7757	3.6564	3.5435	3.4365	3.3351	3.2388	3.1473	11
12	4.2785	4.1274	3.9852	3.8514	3.7251	3.6060	3.4933	3.3868	3.2859	3.1903	12
13	4.3624	4.2028	4.0530	3.9124	3.7801	3.6555	3.5381	3.4272	3.3224	3.2233	13
14	4.4317	4.2646	4.1082	3.9616	3.8241	3.6949	3.5733	3.4587	3.3507	3.2487	14
15	4.4890	4.3152	4.1530	4.0013	3.8593	3.7261	3.6010	3.4834	3.3726	3.2682	15
16	4.5364	4.3567	4.1894	4.0333	3.8874	3.7509	3.6228	3.5026	3.3896	3.2832	16
17	4.5755	4.3908	4.2190	4.0591	3.9099	3.7705	3.6400	3.5177	3.4028	3.2948	17
18	4.6079	4.4187	4.2431	4.0799	3.9279	3.7861	3.6536	3.5294	3.4130	3.3037	18
19	4.6346	4.4415	4.2627	4.0967	3.9424	3.7985	3.6642	3.5386	3.4210	3.3105	19
20	4.6567	4.4603	4.2786	4.1103	3.9539	3.8083	3.6726	3.5458	3.4271	3.3158	20
21	4.6750	4.4756	4.2916	4.1212	3.9631	3.8161	3.6792	3.5514	3.4319	3.3198	21
22	4.6900	4.4882	4.3021	4.1300	3.9705	3.8223	3.6844	3.5558	3.4356	3.3230	22
23	4.7025	4.4985	4.3106	4.1371	3.9764	3.8273	3.6885	3.5592	3.4384	3.3254	23
24	4.7128	4.5070	4.3176	4.1428	3.9811	3.8312	3.6918	3.5619	3.4406	3.3272	24
25	4.7213	4.5139	4.3232	4.1474	3.9849	3.8342	3.6943	3.5640	3.4423	3.3286	25

Table A.2.2 continued

n	31%	32%	33%	34%	35%	36%	37%	38%	39%	40%	n
1	0.7634	0.7576	0.7519	0.7463	0.7407	0.7353	0.7299	0.7246	0.7194	0.7143	1
2	1.3461	1.3315	1.3172	1.3032	1.2894	1.2760	1.2627	1.2497	1.2370	1.2245	2
3	1.7909	1.7663	1.7423	1.7188	1.6959	1.6735	1.6516	1.6302	1.6093	1.5889	3
4	2.1305	2.0957	2.0618	2.0290	1.9969	1.9658	1.9355	1.9060	1.8772	1.8492	4
5	2.3897	2.3452	2.3021	2.2604	2.2200	2.1807	2.1427	2.1058	2.0699	1.9352	5
6	2.5875	2.5342	2.4828	2.4331	2.3852	2.3388	2.2936	2.2506	2.2086	2.1680	6
7	2.7386	2.6775	2.6187	2.5620	2.5075	2.4550	2.4043	2.3555	2.3083	2.2628	7
8	2.8539	2.7860	2.7208	2.6582	2.5982	2.5404	2.4849	2.4315	2.3801	2.3306	8
9	2.9419	2.8681	2.7976	2.7300	2.6653	2.6033	2.5437	2.4866	2.4317	2.3790	9
10	3.0091	2.9304	2.8553	2.7836	2.7150	2.6495	2.5867	2.5265	2.4689	2.4136	10
11	3.0604	2.9776	2.8987	2.8236	2.7519	2.6834	2.6180	2.5555	2.4956	2.4383	11
12	3.0995	3.0133	2.9314	2.8534	2.7792	2.7084	2.6409	2.5764	2.5148	2.4559	12
13	3.1294	3.0404	2.9559	2.8757	2.7994	2.7268	2.6576	2.5916	2.5286	2.4685	13
14	3.1522	3.0609	2.9744	2.8923	2.8144	2.7403	2.6698	2.6026	2.5386	2.4775	14
15	3.1696	3.0764	2.9883	2.9047	2.8255	2.7502	2.6787	2.6106	2.5457	2.4839	15
16	3.1829	3.0882	2.9987	2.9140	2.8337	2.7575	2.6852	2.6164	2.5509	2.4885	16
17	3.1931	3.0971	3.0065	2.9209	2.8398	2.7629	2.6899	2.6202	2.5546	2.4918	17
18	3.2008	3.1039	3.0124	2.9260	2.8443	2.7668	2.6934	2.6236	2.5573	2.4941	18
19	3.2067	3.1090	3.0169	2.9299	2.8476	2.7697	2.6959	2.6258	2.5592	2.4958	19
20	3.2112	3.1129	3.0202	2.9327	2.8501	2.7718	2.6977	2.6274	2.5606	2.4970	20
21	3.2174	3.1158	3.0227	2.9349	2.8519	2.7734	2.6991	2.6285	2.5616	2.4979	21
22	3.2173	3.1180	3.0246	2.9365	2.8533	2.7746	2.7000	2.6294	2.5623	2.4985	22
23	3.2193	3.1197	3.0260	2.9377	2.8543	2.7754	2.7008	2.6300	2.5628	2.4989	23
24	3.2209	3.1210	3.0271	2.9386	2.8550	2.7760	2.7013	2.6304	2.5632	2.4992	24
25	3.2220	3.1220	3.0279	2.9392	2.8556	2.7765	2.7017	2.6307	2.5634	2.4994	25

INDEX